A Political History
of the Olympic Games

Westview Replica Editions

This book is a Westview Replica Edition. The concept of
Replica Editions is a response to the crisis in academic and
informational publishing. Library budgets for books have been
severely curtailed; economic pressures on the university presses
and the few private publishing companies primarily interested in
scholarly manuscripts have severely limited the capacity of the
industry to properly serve the academic and research communities.
Many manuscripts dealing with important subjects, often representing the highest level of scholarship, are today not econom-
ically viable publishing projects. Or, if they are accepted for
publication, they are often subject to lead times ranging from
one to three years. Scholars are understandably frustrated when
they realize that their first-class research cannot be published
within a reasonable time frame, if at all.

Westview Replica Editions are our practical solution to the
problem. The concept is simple. We accept a manuscript in camera-
ready form and move it immediately into the production process.
The responsibility for textual and copy editing lies with the
author or sponsoring organization. If necessary we will advise
the author on proper preparation of footnotes and bibliography.
We prefer that the manuscript be typed according to our speci-
fications, though it may be acceptable as typed for a dissertation or prepared in some other clearly organized and readable
way. The end result is a book produced by lithography and bound
in hard covers. Initial edition sizes range from 400 to 800
copies, and a number of recent Replicas are already in second
printings. We include among Westview Replica Editions only works
of outstanding scholarly quality or of great informational value,
and we will continue to exercise our usual editorial standards
and quality control.

A Political History
of the Olympic Games

David B. Kanin

The turmoil surrounding the 1980 Olympic Games, says
the author, was nothing new--it was merely the most recent,
and most complex, manifestation of the political content of
modern sport. Despite the mythology perpetrated by Olympic
publicists, the modern Olympic Games were founded with expressly political goals in mind and continue to thrive on
ties to global affairs. Political content, insists Kanin,
is not an intrusion on sport from outside--it is a fundamental underpinning of the Olympic system.
   Proceeding from this premise, the author analyzes
each Olympic festival as part of its political and diplomatic environment. He traces the political history of the
Olympic Games from their origins in 1896, examines the 1980
Olympic imbroglio, looks ahead to 1984, and comments on
some proposals for Olympic reform.

As a political analyst for the U.S. Central Intelligence Agency, David B. Kanin has had access to information
enabling him to present a unique perspective on the events
surrounding the 1980 Moscow Olympics and U.S. boycott
effort. In addition to his work with the CIA, he has
taught in the Political Science Departments of Boston College and Framingham State College, both in Massachusetts.

A Political History of the Olympic Games

David B. Kanin

Westview Press / Boulder, Colorado

A Westview Replica Edition

The views expressed in this book are the author's alone; they do not reflect
the opinions of the U.S. Central Intelligence Agency or the U.S. government.

Copyright © 1981 by Westview Press, Inc.

Second printing, 1982

Published in 1981 in the United States of America by
    Westview Press, Inc.
    5500 Central Avenue
    Boulder, Colorado 80301
    Frederick A. Praeger, Publisher

Library of Congress Catalog Card Number 81-4164
ISBN 0-86531-109-9

Printed and bound in the United States of America

Contents

Preface

I will try to make two points in this analysis:
first, that the politics of sport comes from the natural
political content of the modern sport system; second,
that each Olympic Games is an inherently political
event. Dating the "mixing" of politics and the Olympics
from 1908, 1936, or 1972 leaves the impression that once
upon a time the Games were truly free of political
"interference." In fact, despite the mythology of
Olympic publicists, the Olympic Games were founded with
expressly political goals in mind and have thrived on
ties to global affairs. It is no coincidence that the
two Olympiads that were most ignored by politicians, in
1900 and 1904, were also the least successful.

Therefore, calls for the separation of sport and
politics are futile because they are irrelevant. One of
the primary errors of those seeking support for the 1980
Olympic boycott was to give lip service to those calls
rather than repudiate them.

This work investigates a curious slice of history
within its political context. It is not an exhaustive
history of the Games, nor of political sport in general
(the Olympics are only the most famous events in a vast
network of political competitions). Rather, it is an
attempt to apply traditional methods of historical
analysis to a relatively neglected area of concern to
students of politics (as opposed to the trend of applying
overarching "methodology" to traditional areas of interest).

D.B.K.

Glossary

Exposition of the following terms results from a conceptual framework subsuming organized sport in its political context:

PLAY: Play can be defined as activities which are voluntary within limits of time and space with uncertain and unproductive outcomes. Play stands outside ordinary life and yet involves the participant utterly and intensely.[1] Although play stands outside of pragmatic, occupational activities, such action is not necessarily entered into for that purpose; if it is, it is called recreation.[2] Play usually is governed by rules.[3]

Present definitions of play pay great attention to its social aspects. Jean Piaget saw pure play as not involving any conflict.[4] To him, play is the phenomenon of the ego working out its problems; only in its social context can it give rise to the seeds of conflict or competition.

Other authors recognize that play, as a social phenomenon, is part of a hierarchy of leisure activities. Once competition and, perhaps, stakes enter into the equation, scholars must enter the realm of games and sport.[5]

GAME: Games are rulebound and competitive activities in which there are material or psychological stakes to be won or lost as a result of the competition.[6] Roger Callois listed four categories of games: competitive, games of chance, mimicry, and what he described as the pursuit of vertigo--high wire acrobatics or other activities designed to destroy momentarily the stability of perception.[7] Sociological definitions of games tend to stress these activities as evidence of the tendency toward order.[8]

SPORT: There are many definitions of sport and many problems of defining it in its proper political context. The oversimplification of sport as an extension of "game," for example, is a common one. Sport has been described as "a set of rules institutionalized in games, or in any game occurance or event."[9] More elaborate

xi

definitions take the role of sport in society into
account. For Richard Sipes, sport is

> a physical activity (1) engaged in primarily
> for amusement or recreation, (2) with no
> ostensible religious ritual or subsistence-
> activity training significance, and (3)
> involving at least two adult individuals.[10]

This is better, but the extreme youth of the world's
greatest female gymnasts brings maturity into question
as a criterion, and the activities of "Athletes in
Action" certainly link religion and sport. The definition as a whole leaves out the necessary elements of
competition and ruleboundedness. Sport is a rulebound,
competitive set of activities with uncertain outcomes
engaged in for non-occupational purposes. Professional
sport is a contradiction in terms, except regarding
spectators and weekend gamblers.

Sports have histories, rituals, and traditions
attached to them resulting from their organization into
bureaucratic administrative structures. Standardized
measures of performance increase the unity of sport
tradition and maximize the pull of sport across cultural
boundaries. Statistics provide the unity of sport
through time and space.

ATHLETIC: Athletics and sports are usually considered
synonymous. "Athletic" itself comes from a Greek word
meaning prize, and thus stresses the goal of sport--
winning. James Keating once defined the sportsman as
interested in competition and the athlete as interested
only in winning.[11]

Actually, the terms are not really synonymous. In
many parts of the former British Empire, "athletic"
refers specifically to those sports grouped in the United
States under the rubric of "track and field." Athletic
activities are those which require an extraordinary
amount of physical exertion, and thus include those
sports involving such exertion. Chess is a non-athletic
sport, even though players often train for it quite
vigorously.

A growing phenomenon in the athletic world is that
of the athletic exhibition. International tours of
gymnasts and figure skaters often involve purposeful
exclusion of competition in favor of technical or
stylistic display. Such athletics are more in the
realm of circus than sport. Unlike sports, athletics can
be occupational in nature.

CONTEST: To quote Gunther Luschen:

> Contest in sport occurs when at least two
> units (individuals or teams) compete under
> specific rules and agreements, for superiority
> in a non-representative skill or strategy.[12]

This good working definition is marred by the word
"non-representative." Sport may not have anything to do
with the contestants' occupations or real-life activities, but it may be quite representative of organizations
or states in whose names they vie. International sport
organizations propagate the doctrine that the contests
under their jurisdiction are separate from international
politics. Actually, the contestants serve as conscious
national symbols for their respective political systems.
COMPETITION: Competition is the mechanism of sport. It
is the struggle between at least two units for the stakes
of sport using all methods and weapons allowed under the
rules of the particular event. In this way it is
different from conflict, which involves all means available to opponents regardless of the rules of the contest.
Competition is a relationship between at least two
opponents who agree to play within the rules, or between
a human participant and a self-imposed opponent (the
clock, a geographical obstacle, or one's own expecta-
tions). Conflict need not be a relationship if one side
or both struggles for its own goals, according to its
own value system.[13] If the opponent is so reprehensible
that his or her defeat is more important than the fair
struggle in sport, then discreet violation of the rules
may be consciously employed. The intensity of competition and its tendency to spill over into conflict often
blur these terms.
SPORTSMANSHIP: Sportsmanship involves a process of
inculcating the individual with societal values through
the medium of sport participation. Since the "rights"
and "wrongs" of sport are more clearly perceived than
the intricacies of legal jargon and political maneuver,
principles of sportsmanship are effective weapons in the
state's struggle to integrate its people and its doctrines.
SPECTATOR: A spectator is an indirect or vicarious
participant in a sporting event. Followers of sport are
even more important targets of propaganda for national
integration than the athletes themselves. A fan is a
spectator who feels partisan emotion toward at least one
of the contestants in a sporting event. Fan is a
diminutive of fanatic.
Spectators must do more than just view the sporting
event. They must have at least a rudimentary understanding of the rules and the stakes of the contest in
order to induce their vicarious participation.

Spectator sports are dramatic displays of sport for the sake of entertaining masses of people. Winning and losing are more clearly portrayed in sport than in many forms of drama, and the fact that these events are part of the spectator's real life can lead to a violent reaction or a somber depression resulting from the event.

Direct sport consumption involves attendance at the sporting event itself; indirect sport consumption is spectating through television, radio, or other media intermediaries.[14]

NOTES

1. Roger Callois, Man, Play, and Games (Glencoe, Ill.: Free Press, 1961), p. 4, and Larry McNeil, "The Development of a Theory of Sports Competitiveness" (unpublished Ed.D dissertation, North Texas State University, 1971), p. 26.

2. The distinction between work and play is clearer in terms of the verb to play. Sports that evolved out of work activities, such as boating, boxing, or hunting are never "played;" those that have no basis in occupational life are. E. Larrabee and Rolf Meyersohn, ed., Mass Leisure (Glencoe, Ill.: Free Press, 1958), p. 71.

3. Callois, Man, Play, and Games, p. 4.

4. Larrabbe and Meyersohn, ed., Mass Leisure, p. 71.

5. John Talamini and Charles Hines Page, Sport and Society: An Anthology (New York: Little Brown, 1973), p. 43.

6. McNeil, "The Development of a Theory of Sports Competitiveness," p. 26.

7. Callois, Man, Play, and Games, p. 14.

8. Hedwig Keri, "Ancient Games and Popular Games," American Imago, XV, #3 (Spring, 1958), p. 74.

9. Paul Weiss, Sport, A Philosophical Inquiry (Carbondale and Edwardsville, Ill.: Southern Illinois University Press, 1969), p. 142.

10. Richard Sipes, "War, Sports, and Aggression," American Anthropologist, LXXV, #2 (February, 1973), p. 64.

11. James W. Keating, "Sportsmanship as a Moral Category," Ethics, LXXV, #1 (October, 1964), p. 31.

12. Gunther Luschen, "Cooperation, Association, and Contest," Journal of Conflict Resolution, XIV, #1 (March, 1970), p. 21.

13. Thomas Schelling, The Strategy of Conflict (Cambridge, Mass.: Harvard University Press, 1960), pp. 4-5.

14. Barry McPherson, "Socialization and the Role of the Sport Consumer: The Construction and Testing of a Theory and Causal Model" (unpublished Ph.D dissertation, University of Wisconsin, 1972), p. 4.

1 | Introduction

Every four years complaints are heard about the intrusion of politics in the Olympic Games. It seems that, if only the latter could be freed from the former, the beauty of sport and the experience of international contact could contribute to building mutual respect and human understanding. We are told that the international Olympic system idealizes fair play and sportsmanship, and ameliorates struggle, hatred, and petty jealousy through structured competition and institutional goodwill.

In fact, however, international sport thrives on the very politics Olympic publicists decry. Sport organs are structured to maximize political rivalry over the Games or other major sporting events; they are neither more or less "political" than anything else. An analysis of the politics of sport, on the other hand, reveals a specific place for sport in the international system.

SPORT AND POLITICS

International sport is a form of cross-cultural activity which attracts the interest of, and is understood by, a mass public. Most of those involved in sport transactions are indirect participants who have their contact with athletes and fans from other states second hand, via the mass media. Modern communications technology makes màtches of national interest immediately available to anyone who wants to watch or listen. It enables this mass public, which tends to identify with the athletes, to take notice of contests against teams or individuals from friendly or hostile states. Governments can use this identification when sporting events are staged to demonstrate the temper of relations between the states represented by the athletes.

The cancellation of such an activity can also be a risk-free method of expressing displeasure with another country and its policies. The Soviet Union and United States, for example, cancelled several events during the

1

1960s, when both countries wished to express their mutual dislike without losing control over their confrontation.

Sport is safe in this way because it is peripheral to the international system. Sporting activities are simply not as vital as are economic, legal, or diplomatic relations. A defeat in a match will not normally be avenged by the use of force by the state whose athletic representatives have lost. Although sport is an activity organized largely into units corresponding in name and jurisdiction to the state, governments have little control over the rules, equipment, standard, and outcome of play. Yet, even without the direct involvement of state power, the public can be made aware of moods and policies toward other countries.

Unlike many forms of inter-cultural relations, sport is competitive in nature. Art works can be exchanged without necessarily leading to a zero-sum comparision of national heritages. Comparisons between cultures are common, of course, but they are not required by the mechanism of cultural activity itself.

Such comparisions are intrinsic to the nature of international sport. If the staging of a sporting event can be a sign of cooperation, the activity itself is a direct comparison of the physical and mental abilities of the societies' human resources. States may try to use sport to represent international goodwill, but the mechanism of sport makes it a potential forum for inter-state confrontation as well.

Paradoxically, sport is also important in international relations because, as an activity, it has no intrinsic political value. It can be used by any state to demonstrate the physical prowess of the human resources of any ideology or value system. Sport activity has no political content in itself, therefore the sporting process can be given any political interpretation imaginable. The Gentlemen Sportsman, All-American Boy, and New Soviet Man can all play the same sport controlled by the same federation. Sport provides an arena for the direct comparison of athletes representing different societies by spectators who understand rules which are common to most of the world.

The use of sport to convey a diplomatic message or to promote the identification of the citizen with the state and its policies is now a regularized and systematic phenomenon. It is so because the political and technological revolutions of the last two centuries have called for active participation of political "spectators" in most political systems.

PARTICIPATION

The international sport system is divided on the question of credentials for participation. Athletes are loosely defined as "amateur" or "professional" depending on whether or not they take money directly for their participation in sport. There is no single institution which controls all of the world's professional athletes. On the other hand, amateur sport is largely controlled through the Olympic Movement.

The amateur-professional distinction has always been difficult to define, and the growing interest of states and corporations in sport has made it even more so. Some states now subsidize their best athletes, and many companies pay competitors to advertise their products. There are federations, such as the International Association Football Federation (FIFA), that accept professionals in their activities. Only "amateurs" may compete in Olympic soccer competition, but professionals are welcomed by FIFA in the World Cup championships, easily the most popular single international event.

Despite the World Cup, and the relatively recent explosion of professional athletics, the amateur-based Olympic system remains the chief source of political sport transactions. Its organization, ideology, and historical development have provided the main focus for the growth of sport as an important activity in the international system. States permit Olympic institutions to retain control over sport, and tend to base domestic sport programs on some version of the Olympic ideal amended to correspond to stated national goals.

Interstate sport does not always depend on units of the Olympic system for promotion and execution. Bilateral sport exchanges are often arranged through the same diplomatic channels as other forms of cultural and political interactions. But even such events as "Ping Pong Diplomacy" take advantage of the fact that the Olympic system (which includes federations in control of sports not in the Olympic Games) provides states with a representative, yet peripheral forum in which to arrange activities influencing popular perceptions of political moods. The visit of an American table tennis team to China did more to alter public perceptions of US-China relations than any of the other signs leading to President Nixon's trip to Beijing.

THE OLYMPIC SYSTEM

The International Olympic System consists of four parts:

1. The International Olympic Committee
2. National Olympic Committees
3. International Sport Federations
4. Regional Games Federations

These organs control the following events:

1. The Olympic Games have been held every four
   years (except during the two World Wars) since
   1896. Each four year cycle is called an
   "Olympiad," with the Games celebated at the
   end. The Moscow Olympics were the Games of the
   XXII Olympiad. If they had not been held the
   Olympic cycle would still count them as having
   taken place; in any case the 1984 Olympics will
   be those of the XXIII Olympiad. Olympic Winter
   Games, held in the same year, do not hold the
   same designation, since the ancient Greeks had
   no such skiing and skating festivals. Since
   World War II the winter Olympics have been
   awarded separately from the summer (before
   this the summer host had the right of first
   refusal concerning the winter Olympics.)
2. Regional Games are celebrated at four-year
   cycles as well. Each region has its Games in
   a non-Olympic year, following the tradition
   of other ancient Games.
3. World, Regional, and National Championships in
   each sport are held at varying intervals under
   the control of sport federations or of their
   sanctioned national units.

The International Olympic Committee (IOC), founded
in 1894, is still the centerpiece of the Olympic movement. Its founder, Baron Pierre de Coubertin, perceived
the need for a unifying ideology for all sportsmen
(female competition came much later) to preserve the
ideals of sportsmanship and goodwill. He turned to
ancient Olympic tradition and adapted it to postulate the
philosophical unity of mind and body as the model for
future social man. To popularize his ideas he had to
construct an organization which could satisfy the desires
for prestige held by the states and governments to which
he preached.

As the system of sport federations grew, the
functions of the IOC were increasingly limited to the
selection and supervision of Olympic sites and the
perpetuation of its own membership. As the federations
have taken control of the actual mechanism of sport, the
IOC has evolved into a body largely concerned with its
ideology and privileges.

Lausanne was chosen as the site for IOC headquarters in 1913. The IOC President, who is expected to be the leading spokesman for the Olympic movement, chairs a nine-member Executive Board with the assistance of three vice-presidents. The president is elected initially for an eight-year term and can be reelected at subsequent four-year intervals. Executive Board members sit for four year terms.

IOC members are not official representatives of their states, but rather ambassadors of the Olympic ideal in their homelands. Yet, from the beginning, the IOC has reflected the political situation around it. The IOC was born in the era of the "Great Powers" and so these were overrepresented in its membership. Neither the subsequent League or United Nations Assembly models led to any change in that system; Olympic demography continues to reflect, more or less, the prevailing power balance. The superpowers, former Olympic hosts (overwhelmingly white and European), and several other states have more than one member on the IOC. Other countries acquire representation as they gain political independence. The IOC thus has a sort of weighted voting system, similar to that suggested for the UN General Assembly.

The National Olympic Committees (NOCs) are composed of local Olympic officials, representatives of various national sporting bodies (state organs or the local units of sport federations), and persons from other interested government and business agencies. The NOCs are the national representatives of the International Olympic Committee and act for it on all domestic matters. As long as they recognize the supremacy of the IOC and Olympic ideology the NOCs are granted considerable autonomy over local affairs. In order for a national Olympic committee to be recognized by the IOC it must represent a viable political unit with a stable government. The NOC must have international Olympic sanction before its athletes may compete in the Olympic Games. Sport federations have the same power over their own national units.

Although IOC spokesmen bemoan the mixing of sports and politics, the Olympic system almost exactly duplicates the names and territorial jurisdiction of states. In effect, the recognition of a national Olympic committee is tacit recognition of a government and existing boundaries. Those few sub-state units in international sport cling to their separate Olympic status, making use of it in the search for domestic and international legitimacy.

The IOC insists that NOCs be structurally separate from their governments, but makes no complaint if they are under the de facto control of political authorities.

The IOC prefers to bend its own rules rather than risk driving an offending state into forming a rival sport organization, a constant IOC concern.

If a group objects to a certain government a boycott of its athletes provides a means of publicizing opposition in a manner understandable to the largest audience in international politics. Representative assaults on the legitimacy of states, whether through boycott, terror, or propaganda, are possible because the Olympic system is an expression of the political status quo.

No city may submit a bid for the Olympic Games except through its NOC, which also controls national team formation. The IOC allows national Olympic authorities wide lattitude regarding methods of team selection.

When an Olympic member state receives the honor of hosting the Olympic Games, the NOC forms, along with local federation units, government and business agencies, a Games Organizing Committee. The organizing committee is responsible for preparation of the Olympic site. This body also manages the Games themselves, but must conform to federation rules concerning the equipment and conduct of each sport.

The organizing committee must also finance Olympic preparation, and is subject to IOC overview during the long period required to create the Olympic Games. The organizing committee can adjudicate disputes that cannot be settled under specific IOC guidelines and can sometimes add sports to the Olympic program.

The NOCs serve to guard the purely political character of the Olympic movement. Only those wearing state colors may participate in the Olympic Games, and NOCs usually insist that their teams include only citizens of the country in question. The teams, once chosen, march in the opening Olympic ceremony behind the state flag. Olympic victors are usually saluted to the strains of their national anthems.* No individuals may compete in the Olympics outside the prevailing political framework of international sport.

NOCs have gradually increased their say in Olympic politics, but have had to protect themselves from IOC protection of its fading prerogatives. A few NOCs from each continent gather periodically in an umbrella Association of Olympic Committees, but the attempt to unite in a Permanent General Assembly of NOCs foundered

---

*Refusal to do this by West European teams was a serious blow to Moscow's Olympic policy, which was based on attracting representative political displays.

after effective IOC exploitation of disputes among NOC
officials themselves.

Each sport is under the control of an International
Sport Federation. Some of these are older than the IOC
itself, but all have grown and prospered through
association with the Olympic system. The federations
legislate standards for equipment and athletic programs.
In addition, they choose all referees and control
participation by defining the word "amateur" as they
wish. While all parts of the Olympic system insist that
only amateurs may participate in the Olympic Games, this
word continues to be as difficult to define as "aggression," and the enormous financial benefits offered to
athletes and their federations by governments and
corporations make the term increasingly meaningless.
Once, in exasperation, IOC President Avery Brundage
threatened to throw alpine skiing out of the Olympic
system because he alleged that the International Ski
Federation was guilty of some special venality in the
Karl Schranz case. In fact, the publicity of the incident publicized the general commercial domination of
sport, and Brundage's eventual failure to make his word
stick reflected the continuing decline of IOC authority.

The federations are represented on IOC special
commissions dealing with contemporary Olympic problems
such as drugs, the Olympic Academy (at which the word
"politics" is excised from the curriculum), and ideology.
Federations have the same jurisdictional tug-of-war with
the IOC as national Olympic committees, so they meet
together in a General Assembly of International
Federations, an increasingly influential body in international sport.

The international sport federations are also
influential in Regional Games Federations. The regional
games can be as politically important as the Olympics,
since regional powers can display their sporting talent
without competition from the rest of the world.

The events controlled by federations have as much
political content as the Olympic Games. World, Regional,
and National championships exist in the same system and
are subject to the same considerations of legitimacy,
propaganda, and prestige. The following pages use the
Olympics to represent the sport system as a whole, and
Olympic politics should not be seen as the sum of
politics in sport.

In dealing with competition and politics in sport,
the body of this book leaves out most of those events
that go beyond Olympic and legal rules into the realm of
conflict. Violence and sport have a special relationship, one which approaches the issue of sport and human
maturation from a different perspective than ordinary
political sport, even though all political sport exists
in the same organizational framework.

2

The Olympic Revival

Transnational relations are international transactions in which at least one of the participants is not
a state or governmental organ (defining this term is
often made a complicated affair, but it really boils
down to this). It is clear that the revolution in
transportation and communication technologies in the
past hundred years has caused an explosion of such inter-
changes, but it is not so clear that this has led to a
fundamental transformation of the international system
(as opposed to the mechanisms by which that system
works).

The views of those who feel that international
politics have changed radically are represented by those
espousing functionalism and others arguing against
"trilateralism" and transnational imperialism. David
Mitrany and Ernst Haas believed that an expanding web of
technical and economic organizations, by providing vital
international services,would (Mitrany) or might (Haas)
lead to voluntary surrender of state sovereignty in a
world structured according to rational coordination.

Giovanni Arrighi,[1] on the other hand, has suggested
that transnationalism is the stage following monopoly
capitalism, leading to a new form of imperialism
succeeding Lenin's empire of finance capital. Multi-
lateral corporations castrate the state by superceding
its functions and its law.

Neither of these extremes, nor the exercises in
between, concentrate on organizations created to cross
cultures rather than borders. There are many studies on
the workings of these structures themselves, but few
which weave them into a global pattern with states and
companies.

The Olympic system involves both states and busi-
nesses, each of which profits through the banking of
money, prestige, and political legitimacy. There is no

overall tug-of-war between state and company; there is a
place for each in an Olympic movement that cannot survive
without both.

Olympic celebation is the showcase of a system
pervasive in international politics. The Games provide
an outlet for any international actor willing and able to
use them to attract attention. This work concentrates on
the political rather than commercial aspect of this
process in line with the author's belief that the state
will remain the most important actor in international
relations for the foreseeable future.

The international Olympic system is among the oldest
of transnational organizations; it began to function a
quarter of a century before the founding of the League
of Nations. Most of those institutions which preceded
it, such as the Universal Postal Union and the antecedent
organs of the International Telecommunications Union,
were created to carry out vital international functions
more efficiently than could be done by states themselves
(thus nicely fitting the functionalist model). Others,
such as the Red Cross, provided the same services for
humanitarian purposes, particularly in wartime situations
when states needed well-trained and impartial personnel
to see to the needs of citizens captured or wounded in
battle (Amnesty International attempts to serve the same
function for citizens held by their own states).

The Olympic movement became the first such organization to carry out intercultural functions not really
required by the evolving international political system.
Ironically, this is precisely the basis for the political
importance of international sport. It soon began to
serve as public reinforcement of the myths of Western
civilization within a system encouraging adaptation to
those myths by emerging national movements and by post-
colonial rulers. Third world leaders still seek in sport
a means of imposing Western-style political borders and
legal constraints on non-Western cultural bases.

Though many leaders of the Olympic Movement look to
the heritage of ancient Greece for inspiration as to the
ideals of sport, the political roots of the modern sport
system are to be found in the historical development of
modern Europe. Both the ideology and institutions of the
Olympic movement were products of the Europe that emerged
from the period following the French Revolution. If the
eighteenth century was an era when elites believed in the
efficacy of "rational "approaches to political manage-
ment, the nineteenth and twentieth have been dominated by
emotional mobilization of the masses (despite the efforts
of social science to turn the clock backward).

Four factors led to the creation of the Olympic
system as part of international politics: the tradition
of the ancient Games and the interest aroused in them

by nineteenth century archaeologists, the European
exercise movement and its national implications, English
sport and the English public school system under the
influence of Thomas Arnold, and the personal will and
determination of Baron Pierre de Coubertin.

THE ANCIENT OLYMPICS

The ancient Greeks considered their Games to be of
enormous political as well as religious and social
significance. At their height, before the decline of
the Greek city-state system, only "Greeks" (defined in
terms of linguistic, religious, and ethnic orientation)
were allowed to participate.
Many Greeks considered the first recorded Olympiad
(776 B.C.) the beginning of history. The Olympic cycle
was the basis for the Greek calendar, which ran in much
the same quadrennial fashion that is now used to count
modern Olympiads.
The Olympics were the most prestigious of several
forms of athletic celebration; the others having national
prestige were the Pythian, Nemean, and Isthmian Games.
Solon provided a measure of the relative importance of
these activities, offering 500 drachmas to a victor at
Olympia but only a 100 to an Isthmian champion.[2]
Although the athletes did not compete under their
cities' flags, units of the Greek political system
did bask in the glory of their Olympic victors. Only
the winner was celebrated; each Olympiad was recorded
in the name of the man who won it.[3] According to
Pausanius, only those who won ever had their likenesses
immortalized in statues at Olympia.[4] Olympic champions
were also celebrated by leading poets of the day. The
victor's city would often pay for an ode which would
celebrate the town as much as the athlete.
Olympic heroes were feasted at public expense. If
taken prisoner in battle the Olympic victor would be
released, if killed his enemies would erect a monument
to him.[5] At times athletes were bought away from one
city in order to compete for another (somewhat like
contemporary baseball, only the losing city would be
likely to ban the defector for life).
The ancient Games thus led to the single-minded
adulation of the victor. Pindar's words for the losers
were not as gallant as those which would come from a
modern Olympic publicist. He compared their lot to
Aristomena of Aegina, a Pythian champion:

> And now four times you came down with bodies
> beneath you
> --You meant them harm--
> To whom the Pythian feast have given
> No glad homecoming like yours.

They, when they meet their mothers
Have no sweet laughter around them, moving delight.
In back streets, out of their enemies' way
They cower; for disaster has bitten them.[6]

Pindar often coupled the athlete and the political
condition of his city. Aristomena was a late cause of
celebration in a declining political entity. Aegina was
in the process of being eclipsed by neighboring Athens
when Pindar comforted it with odes to athletic victors.
Thebes was another city of mixed political fortunes
given the same treatment. Pindar's poem in celebration
of the 74th Olympiad (484 B.C.) sang of Heracles as a
Theban.[7] In 457 B.C. the victory of Strepiacles of
Thebes coincided with that of Thebes itself at the battle of Tanagra. Pindar used the opportunity to praise
the glory of the city in both sport and war.[8]
At times Greek politicians used the Games to
demonstrate their city's--and their own--importance. In
416 B.C., during the Peloponesian War, Alcibiades of
Athens entered enough teams of chariots to win first,
second, and fourth places at Olympia.[9]
The ancient Olympics were, therefore, somewhat
similar to the modern version in that political content
was institutionalized in a system which allowed for the
worship of the victor and the celebration of his homeland through his exploits. The idea of competition for
its own sake was an invention of Coubertin and those
who believe that sport could be an agent of human[10]
moral development. They saw international sport as an
extension of chivalry and insisted that "politics" could
only be an intrusion on the athletic process.
Coubertin and his followers used the archaeological
discoveries of the nineteenth century to draw attention
to the Olympic "idea." The excavations at Troy whetted
the appetites of those who next organized digs at
Olympia. Curtius' explorations of the area, sponsored
by the German government, resulted in a greater understanding of the religious and political importance of
the ancient Games. Publicists and academicians such as
Knapp (1881) spread the work of earlier scholars like
Krause (1838) and increased the number of people aware
of the recent discoveries. The classical heritage now
became a reality for people who had thought it was all
a myth.
When Winckelman's lectures in 1852 called attention
to the ancient Olympics Greek patriots themselves became
interested in the idea of an Olympic revival.[11] Greece,
even after independence, was still in a struggle to
expand to what it considered its natural frontiers.
This meant not only opposing the Turks, but also the

rival national aspirations of Serbs and Bulgars. This
political Olympic appeal was designed to increase the
national awareness of the Greek people and to hold the
sympathy of those Western philhellenes already convinced
of the nobility of Greek civilization.[12]

The will of Evangelios Zappas left funds with which
the Greek government financed an "Olympic Games" in
1859. The event was not very successful. John Lucas
described some of the chaos that marred this "Olympiad:"

> Spectators were trampled on and injured by mounted
> police trying to keep the streets open to contes-
> tants, and athletes were arrested for acting like
> spectators. Boys and old men entered the competi-
> tion at the least minute and actually ran in some
> of the preliminary heats in order to get by police
> lines.[13]

Another "Olympiad," in 1875, coincided with an
expedition by Curtius to Greece. Even though unsuccessful, the political lesson of these events would serve
as the model for the Greek government in hosting the
1896 Olympics. This revival of ancient Greek traditions,
however, was not enough to create an international sport
system. Independently of the Greeks, and of Coubertin,
other national heritages found outlets in exercises and
athletic competition.

NATIONAL SPORT

Long before Coubertin organized the International
Olympic Committee, national athletic movements used sport
as a lever in national and international relations.
Sport was merely one of many cultural tools in the physical and ideological mobilization of the masses under the
banner of nationalism. The revival of national literature, for example, was so loaded with political implications that it sometimes had to be done secretly. The
Philike Hetaira encouraged the study of Greek literature
as well as risings against the Turks. Later in the
century the Greeks found themselves in the position of
opposing Bulgarian literacy as much as Bulgarian claims
to Macedonia. For Germans, Grimm's Fairy Tales served
much the same purpose in that a guise that is still
mistaken for children's stories.

Both rulers and ruled perceived exercise to be a
method of training and disciplining the human resources
of national movements. It was used with the most fervor
in an early eighteenth century attempt by Father
Friedrich Ludwig Jahn to wield a national fighting force
in Prussia. This Prussian patriot sought to unify his

people with the kind of national fury he thought necessary in order to defeat Napoleon. His Burschenschaften brought Prussian students together in organizations designed to raise their German consciousness and to nurture intense Francophobia.[14] The Frei Korps were grass roots para-military formations created to give Prussia a version of the "nation-in-arms," and to pressure the weak King Friedrich Wilhelm III into opposing the French.

Father Jahn spread his doctrines through gymnastic societies called Turnvereine. The first of these was organized in 1810 and within a short time the movement spread across Prussia. National consciousness was the political purpose behind strenuous physical exercise and the practice of compulsory gymnastic forms. The Turnvereine were only in their infancy when Napoleon was defeated. Father Jahn then turned his attention to the creation of a German state with Prussia at its head. Turnkunst survived his death in 1852 and flourished in organizations that used gymnastics to train people to fight for the Fatherland.

For a long time the Prussian government opposed this pressure. The concept of "nation" was still considered revolutionary throughout much of Europe. Any movement which based political legitimacy on popular foundations instead of on dynastic privilege was suspect in the eyes of elites. Jahn himself often faced government restriction of his activities, and the first all-German Turnfest was not held until 1860.[15] After 1871 and the absorption of nationalism by the Bismarckian Reich, however, the Turnvereine were embraced by offical publicists of German integration. The movement expanded to embrace even those Germans who were not in the new Germany.[16] "Turner" clubs sprang up in several American cities during the period of great German migration to the United States. Indeed, German refugees introduced Father Jahn's system to the US as early as the 1820's.[17] Turnkunst was one method of keeping German consciousness alive in many of the people who some feared would be lost to the Reich forever.

The connection with German communities in Europe and America was the only important international development of this movement. It was too exclusively Germanic in ideology to attract many people in other countries. In any case the adherents of Father Jahn cared little for the spread of their system to other cultures.

If the exclusive nationalism of the Turnvereine prevented them from becoming the basis for an international athletic system, the exercises they developed could be used in a more universal application. Some Germans, opposed to Father Jahn, removed the harsher aspects of his regimen and taught the system to other Europeans. In addition, Swedish and Danish educators became interested in gymnastics and brought forms of physical exercise to their own peoples.

In Bohemia, Dr. Miroslav Tyrs and Jindrich Fugner adapted the Father Jahn model to the needs of the Czech nation. The Sokol (Falcon) Movement organized Czechs into gymnastic and educational societies. Tyrs sought to create a national identity through national cultural organization. He saw Bohemia as a nation which needed to be awakened from its centuries-old lethargy by means of physical culture and the revival of Czech cultural tradition. Tyrs gave the movement its rallying cry, "He who is a Czech is a Sokol."[18] He urged his followers to keep political goals in mind while exercising their bodies: "Let us serve our nation, it is the noblest of our efforts."[19] The Sokols originally supported the so-called "trialist" approach to the problems of Slavic political aspirations in the Austro-Hungarian setting. This concept envisioned Slavs gaining equality with Germans and Hungarians, creating political autonomy within an economic and security unit tied together by the Habsburg dynasty. How Czechs (West Slavs) Serbs, and Croats (South Slavs) would divide power remained unclear. It was only in 1914, at the outset of World War I, that Sokol leaders joined Thomas Masaryk's call for outright Czech independence.

There was thus a well organized European sport tradition independent of the Olympic idea as Greeks, Germans, and Czechs demonstrated how to use physical education to advance one's own national goals. The Sokols contributed an important step to this process when they put on displays in several European capitals in order to advertise Czech national feeling. They showed other national groups the value of political discipline through sport. When the Olympic system was organized its units continued to use physical display to promote national prestige.

THE ENGLISH SYSTEM

But these forms of exercise did not serve as the athletic basis of the Olympic revival. It was the English who organized many of the most popular forms of modern sport and exported them around the world. Along with these activities went much of the mythology which found its way into the present athletic system. The common rules and standards which made sport an international phenomenon also originated, in large part, in England.

After the Glorious Revolution (1688) the type of sport which later made up the Olympic Movement took permanent root, as did a system of rigid class discrimination. Boxing, for example, became an aristocratic form, while football and wrestling were reserved for the lower classes.[20] The sport which involved the most multi-class participation was horse racing, where most levels of society could serve as gamblers and spectators.[21]

It was not until the nineteenth century, however, that these activities became looked upon as essential to the training of the English child. Physical exertion was the heart of the educational system introduced at that time by Thomas Arnold (nephew of Matthew Arnold).

Arnold, as headmaster at Rugby, formulated a program whereby sport not only became an accepted, but almost an obligatory part of the preparation of the English upper classes. Arnold saw school at the first chapter in a person's social life. He believed sport to be a good method of bringing the adult world to the youth in good working order.[22] Sport and vigorous free play made boys into healthy men, and thus units of a healthy social body. Coubertin himself visited Oxford and came to admire the Arnoldian system.

During his lifetime Arnold merely lay the theoretical foundation for the athletic system constructed by his pupils and successors. In 1837 the Crick Run at Rugby inaugurated cross-country running. There were sprints and steeple chases at Eton in 1845. The Exeter Athletic Club at Oxford was formed in 1850.[23]

Amateurs were strictly separated from professionals. Only the former were given credit for using sport as a character-building method to train for future life. Professionals supposedly were morally bogged down in their sport for the sake of profit. In the classic English system was also a third group, "Gentlemen Sportsmen" who were distinguished purely by class background and who were holdovers from feudal life. The English system promoted both sexual and social rigidity. Sport was all male, and the men were always conscious of their relative social position.[24]

It was the English system of sport, not that of the continent, which spread around the world. In 1810 Lord Byron swam the Bosporus, an event which is still spoken of as an inspiration for modern forms of competitive swimming.[25] The Secretariat of the British delegation at the Congress of Vienna played cricket and attempted to entice other representatives into learning the game. No converts were reported.[26]

Soon, however, English sport became popular throughout the British Empire, the United States, and Europe itself. One sport most representative of this process was football, both in its Association and Rugby Union forms.

There had been attempts to organize this old sport in the period before 1848, but it was only in that year

16

that Trinity College, Harrow, Rugby, Winchester, and
Shrewsbury came together to agree on the Cambridge
Rules.[27] In the next decade and a half interest in
organized football spread away from the schools into
London, where the Football Association was formed in
1863 at Freemason's Tavern.[28] Some natives from the
colonies learned the sport at English schools, while
those who stayed home were taught by British garrisons
and the crews of the Royal Navy. The popularity of
Association Football wherever it was played and the
common "soccer" background of most of the game's teachers
led to the standarization of rules in this sport wherever
it was played. In this way there was establishment of
a basis for common understanding of an intercultural
activity in all parts of the world. Colonial sides
began to play against the English in the 1880's.

Soccer also reached the continent. German students
at Luneberg College accepted the rules of the Association
in 1875, and the game spread across a Germany learning
to organize many sports. The first German side visited
England in 1899, one year after the first match between
German and French footballers.[29] Hungary developed its
own teams after Charlie Lowenrosen brought the first
football into the country in 1896 (the ball was put on
display at the national Hungarian millennial celebration
in Budapest).[30] The first Austro-Hungarian contest was
staged in 1901.

A transnational web was thus already formed by the
time the International Association Football Federation
(FIFA) was created in 1904. The French encouraged the
creation of an international organization while the
English, at first, were reluctant to accept it.[31] The
English were proud of having invented the game and did
not want to be merely one among equals. They finally
complied, just as they would have to get used to the
spread abroad of soccer supremacy.

The other form of football, rugby, had its inception
at the birth of the Association in 1863. Ruggers wanted
to carry the ball, while soccer players insisted on
kicking it. Rugby tended to remain a more elite activity, and did not gain the popular base of the Association.
Rugby did spread to Europe, though never to the extent
that soccer did. Rugby was first played in Germany in
1873, several years before soccer.[32] But the latter was
better organized and more adaptable to mass sport organization in the tradition of the Turnvereine, and was a
key to the German Social-Democratic Party (SPD) method
of keeping its members entertained. It was the organized
transnational nature of soccer, as well as its accept-
ability among all social classes, that caused it to
become the most popular sport in the world. The first
national rugby match between England and Germany was not
played until 1930.[33]

Rugby did find fertile ground in some parts of the Empire. South Africans and New Zealanders, for example, became engrossed in the sport. In New Zealand rugby was a means by which native Maori tribesmen became social-ized into the Empire. Fiji also took up rugby, and there it is is still the national sport.

Britain was acknowledged as the birthplace of modern sport, and in the early days was unchallenged in its play. In many activities, however, the English eventu-ally found keen competition in the United States. The Americans were the first to train themselves for sport in as disciplined a manner as the English. Some of the latter expressed dissatisfaction with the Americans for their tendency to train for the sake of sport, rather than for the development of mature and responsible social beings. The _Times_ of London expressed this view after Oxford defeated Harvard in 1869 in the first rowing contest between the two:

> The victory was a victory of education and the advantage was all on our side. We live--not in rowing alone--a closer life. The competition is sharper. The lessons of the past are more search-ing and more exact.[34]

The _Times_ also betrayed, at this point, the national identification inherent in international sport. Even in its embryonic stages international athletic competi-tion was recognized to excite national passion. The following was a lighthearted reaction to the presence of such feelings during the event:

> It is terrible to think how many millions of pa-triot would have gone to bed with aching hearts... to renew in painful dreams the bitter memories of the national disgrace, if Harvard had beaten Oxford. The surrender of BURGOYNE or CORNWALLIS, the reluctant recognition of the United States, becomes a trifle in comparison to what our defeat would have been.[35]

The rivalry was felt more keenly when the _America_ sailed home with the cup which now bears her name. The early races between English and American yachts were tests of ship design in an age when sail was still a strategic commodity. Anglo-American contests were also heated in track and field events, sports soon to become the staple of the Olympic Games. What the British still call "athletics" was to be the catalyst for continuation of the trans-atlantic rivalry in the early Olympiads.

The first transnational races were contested by
individual champions who would cross the Atlantic to
challenge local favorites or to win meets organized in
the rival country. In track and field organization
followed, rather than preceded, transnational relations,
but once formed tended to control the activity. The
British Amateur Athletic Association was formed in 1880
out of several rival groups and included amateurs of
all classes. The term "Gentleman Sportsman" began to
lose its meaning. Two Americans participated in the
first AAA meet in 1881. The 1888 AAA meet was entered
by eleven Americans in four events.[36]

In the United States track and field also became
the province of organized bodies. The Manhattan
Athletic Club administered American representation at
both the British and French games of 1891.[37] In 1894
Oxford and Yale staged the first transnational inter-
collegiate athletic meet.[38] Track and field was organized
only shortly before the creation of the International
Olympic Committee and the first Olympic Games, held in
1896, were among the earliest of international track and
field meets.[39]

England and the United States were also involved in
the first international polo and water polo matches.
Indeed, sport became such an Anglo-American preoccupation
that it was suggested that an Anglo-Saxon Olympic
Movement be formed.[40] In 1895 J. Ashley Cooper
suggested that athletic contests should serve as the
basis for closer Anglo-American relations. He urged
that Britain choose an American alliance at a time when
"Splendid Isolation" was beginning to appear worn at the
edges. Cooper wanted competition planned in art, literature, and industry, as well as sport. Cooper was
interested in a businesslike exposition to be held every
four years and financed by national and imperial scholar-
ships.[41] Sport would have been merely a side show;
Cooper wanted to bring the English-speaking peoples
together through meetings of their entrepreneurial
classes. Cooper's plan was consistant with the ethnic
exclusivity of ancient Greece, and would have been as
faithful a descendent of that tradition as the system
that emerged in its place.

The Olympic Movement, however, was to be more global
in nature. The English had exported the rules of sport
around the world, but now Baron Pierre de Coubertin, a
French educator, became caught up in the Olympic myth.
While the English system was the one he admired and
adapted for international purposes, it was his response
to the lethargy of the French educational system that
made the Olympic Movement possible.

COUBERTIN

After 1870 France was an uncertain power; its
leaders were in a state of depression and anxious about
the future. It was isolated diplomatically and looked
across the Rhine at a Germany whose power, population,
and vitality were leaving France far behind.
Traditional French education was exclusively
concerned with affairs of the mind. Many believed that
physical exercise took away from mental development.
Despite reforms late in the period of the Second Empire,
France had much less of a physical culture movement than
did Germany or Britain.
The crushing defeat by the Prussians and the poor
international position that followed triggered a serious
reexamination of French culture and of the French nation
itself. As part of this reassessment, the Third Republic
authorized gymnastics clubs formed on the basis of the
German model. Exercise was to be used in a program to
maximize the efficiency of scarce human resources.
France believed itself faced with a perennial
demographic problem; its population was static while
that of Germany was steadily increasing. If France was
to be burdened with fewer people they had to well-
developed and capable of taking care of themselves.
Laws were passed in 1872, 1880, and 1887 which ordered
compulsory gymnastic programs in French schools.[42]
Not content with this, reformers prodded the government to intensify study of educational systems in
other countries. In response to this pressure, Coubertin
was appointed to examine education abroad and to make
recommendations concerning the future of the French
system. Coubertin, the founder of "L'Union des Sports
Athletiques," undertook his mission from 1889-1892.[43]
Coubertin, who was also Secretary of the French
Educational Reform System, soon made it clear that he
wanted to shift the emphasis of French education. He
rejected the German system in favor of Thomas Arnold's.[44]
From a moral and social point of view Coubertin found the
German system to be too militaristic, and inclined toward
the inculcation of military values in impressionable
adolescents. Stating that "the muscles are made to do
the work of a moral educationer,"[45] Coubertin took up a
debate with those who wanted to copy precisely those
values of the German system that he abhored.
Coubertin, who was an Anglophile in any case, saw
the German athletic system as part of the German menace.
He perceived the English program, on the other hand, to
be a moral hope for mankind. He arranged for the first
French crew to row in the Henley Regatta in 1891,[46] and
supervised early Franco-English football matches. He
wanted to use sport to strengthen French moral fiber,

not merely to increase the power of individual Frenchmen
on their way to a war with Germany.

Coubertin travelled to many countries to examine
their exercise systems. He was especially impressed
with sport in the United States, which he called "a
better England."[47] He questioned educators on what
sports they played, which social classes played them
and how often, and in general how important physical
education was perceived in their societies.[48] It was
on this trip that he tried to influence other educators
with his ideas on the use of sport as an international
peacemaker. If sport could develop the human character
and initiate the individual to a more healthy social
life, then people all over the world could be socialized
into roles compatible with the ideal of universal
community. Due to the spread of standarized rules by
the English, sport could serve as a global method of
teaching human understanding. Athletics could become a
unique element in world culture because sport could
become common to all peoples in both form and content.

The implication of this was that if play had to be
standard control had to be central. If sport was to be
a basis for human understanding everyone had to be
liable to the same rules and referees, as well as to the
same ideals.

Coubertin perceived the need for a unifying ideology
for all sports people to give transnational sport its
basis for loyalty from all the world's athletes. He
found the answer in the ancient Olympic tradition that
had drawn attention to the nobility assigned by
Philhellenes to the ancient Greeks. The noble ancient
was to be the model for future social man. Coubertin's
program focused on the individual athlete, rather than
on any state or other form of political organization.
It was in the character of each youth that he placed his
hope for the future. With his sights set well above
France itself, Coubertin presented his ideas to the
French government for consideration in 1892. "Let us,"
as he said,

> export our oarsmen, our runners, our fencers, into
> other lands. That is the true free trade of the
> future; and the day it is introduced into Europe
> the cause of peace will have received a new and
> strong ally.[49]

This was very different from the educational reform
system Coubertin had been commissioned to create, and
his Olympic mythology was greeted coldly by the French
government. So he took his "free trade of the future"
ideas abroad and attempted to sell them to the various
athletic associations of Europe and the United States.

He presented his movement as a basis for the end of
international discord, yet offered the athletes the
opportunity to test themselves in direct competition with
other national representatives. He apparently did not
perceive that athletes would represent states in the
minds of spectators and government leaders and would
provide another form of international rivalry, rather
than serve to diminish it.

His appeals were to national sporting associations
in the process of gaining control over national sport.
He offered them the chance to band together to create
order on the international level in the same way each
was doing in individual countries. His Olympic ideology
provided a cover for what would become an international
athletic oligarchy. To attract existing states and
associations, Coubertin had to provide them with a format
that they could use to increase their prestige. From
the beginning, the Olympic Games were to be vehicles by
which state policy could be expressed. The nationalism
of modern Greek, German, and Bohemian models was as much
a part of international sport as was any system of
Olympic ideals. Each state could display its youth, and
nations such as the Czechs and Finns could demonstrate
their strength without having to incur significant
political or military reprisals from their imperial
masters.

The importance of international politics in transnational sport was demonstrated at the founding meeting
of the International Olympic Committee (IOC), which
Coubertin organized in Paris in 1894. As the chief
territorial revisionists in Europe, the French were not
interested in an organization which would celebrate the
status quo. At one point the French Gymnastics Union
threatened to boycott the affair if any Germans were
allowed to attend.[50] As it was, German organizations
were not represented; the only German at the meeting
was Baron von Reiffenstein acting as an individual.

Once this conclave came to order some representatives expressed strong opposition to the domination of
English sporting forms.[51] These included the French and
Belgians, who recoiled at the implication of the superiority of this form of English culture. "English sports,"
however, were the most universally known, and their
proposed use as the basis of the Olympic Games carried
the day. Coubertin himself continued to stress the
superiority of the English system. He insisted that
although the Greeks were important for the sake of
tradition, the English were really responsible for the
revival of athletics.[52]

The Congress (and Coubertin) chose the first members
of the IOC. These fifteen aristocrats and academicians
were not supposed to be representatives of states, but

rather Olympic ambassadors charged with the responsibility for promotion of the Olympic Movement within
their homelands. However, while the IOC recognized no
political authority, delegates from great powers had
more voting strength than those from smaller states.
The national components of the new Olympic system maintained their independence, an aspect of the Movement
that would grow with the development of transnational
sport. Thus established, the IOC went about the task
of choosing a site for the First Olympiad.

Coubertin had hoped to revive the Games in Paris in
1900, but two aspects of his ideology altered his plans.
First, his Anglophile sentiments alientated many in his
own country; some Frenchmen were suspicious of his
motives and few Frenchment helped him get his games to
Paris.

Second, his use of Greek tradition in advertising
the Games gave Greek nationalists the opportunity to
draw attention to that beleaguered and impoverished
country. The first IOC President was Greek, and the
Greek royal family actively sought the Olympic award.
Although clearly interested in dynastic prestige as
much as in the glory of sport, the Greeks won their
point. The first Olympic Games were scheduled for Athens
in 1896.

In keeping with ancient tradition the Olympic Games
were to be numbered consecutively and celebrated every
four years. The Greeks wanted the Olympic award to be
permanent, but the various federations and Coubertin
himself made it clear that prestige would be alternated
among IOC member countries.[53] The tradition was thus
established whereby each state could vie for the
political prestige of an Olympic award.

Coubertin had tried to graft the English system of
athletics to the international system. To tie this into
a global package he sought to invoke the ancient glories
that many assumed were the legacy of Olympic tradition
and more recent theories concerning the use of sport as
a tool in human moral development. From the beginning,
however, Coubertin was abandoned by his movement. While
arguments that Coubertin was merely a militarist are too
simplistic (and basically inaccurate), Evangelios Zappas
and J. Ashley Cooper were more in line with the Olympic
spirit than was the IOC founder. Nations had learned
from Father Jahn and Miroslav Tyrs how to use sport for
purposes of national rejuvination. All that Coubertin
accomplished was the creation of an umbrella under which
different states could promote their own brand of
athletic achievement. Since sport is, by definition,
competitive, states were provided a forum that promoted
the comparison of different countries' human resources.

From the first, the losers had to stand at attention while the champion's state flag was raised to the strains of a national anthem.

NOTES

1.   Giovanni Arrighi, The Geometry of Imperialism (London: New Left Books, 1976).
2.   Hugh Harlan, History of the Olympic Games, Ancient and Modern (Los Angeles: Bureau of Athletic Research, 1932), p. 15.
3.   Maurice Bogney, "The Olympic Games Today and Yesterday," The Living Age, CCCXXI (May 10, 1924), p. 950.
4.   Pausanius, Description of Greece, trans. by J.G. Frazer (2 vol. London: MacMillan, 1913), p. 310.
5.   Bill Henry, An Approved History of the Olympic Games (New York: G.P. Putnam's Sons, 1948), p. 18.
6.   C.M. Bowra, Pindar (London: Oxford University Press, 1964), p. 182.
7.   Pindar, The Olympian and Pythian Odes, ed. by Basil L. Gildersleeve (New York: Harper, 1885), p. 212.
8.   Pindar, The Isthmian Odes, ed. by J.B. Bury (Amsterdam: Adolf M. Hakkert, 1965), p. 20.
9. Bowra, Pindar, p. 177.
10. Women were not allowed to compete in the ancient Games. If caught, even as spectators, they could be killed. During an Olympic celebation they were barred from Olympia, although this rule was not enforced at all times.
11.   John A. Lucas, "Baron Pierre de Coubertin and the Formative Years of the Modern International Olympic Movement" (Ed.D. dissertation, University of Maryland, 1962), p. 17.
12.   For an elaboration of the Philhellene phenomenon, see W. St. Clair, That Greece Might Be Free: The Philhellens in War of Independence (London: Oxford University Press, 1972).
13.   Lucas, "Baron Pierre de Coubertin...," p. 18.
14.   Frederick Hertz, The German Public Mind in the Nineteenth Century (London: George Allen and Unwin Ltd., 1974), p. 228.
15.   R. Harbott, Olympia und die Olympischen Spiele von 776 B.C. bis Heute (Berlin: Whilhelm Limpert Verlag, 1935), p. 76.
16.   Arno Breitmeyer and P.G. Hoffman, Sport und Staat (Hambuurg: Broschek, 1934), p. 25.
17.   R.H. Boyle, Sport, Mirror of American Life (Boston: Little Brown and Co., 1963), p. 11.
18.   Ladislav Jandacek, "The Sokol Movement in Czechoslovakia," The Slavonic Review, XI, #31 (July, 1932), p. 71.

24

19. R.W. Seton-Watson, History of the Czechs and Slovaks (Hamden, Conn.: Archon Books, 1965), p. 213.
20. Joseph Strutt, The Sports and Pastimes of the People of England, ed. by J.W. Howe (London: Chatto and Windus, 1898), p. 22.
21. Reuel Denney, The Astonished Muse (Chicago: University of Chicago Press, 1957), p. 98.
22. Lucas, "Baron Pierre de Coubertin," p. 49.
23. Melvin Watman, History of British Athletics (London: Robert Hale, 1968), pp. 17-18.
24. Paul Hoch, Rip Off the Big Game: The Exploitation of Sports by the Power Elite (Garden City N.Y.: Doubleday, 1972), p. 47.
25. Josef Veto, ed., Sports In Hungary (Budapest: Corvina Press, 1965), p. 61.
26. Phillip Goodhart and Christopher Chataway, War Without Weapons (London: W.H. Allen, 1968), p. 35.
27. R.W. Pickford, "The Psychology of the History and Organization of Association Football," British Journal of Psychology, XXXI, #2 (October, 1940), p. 84.
28. Ibid.
29. Breitmeyer and Hoffman, Sport und Staat, p. 35.
30. Veto, Sports in Hungary, p. 44.
31. Pickford, "Association Football," p. 84.
32. L.S. Weir, Europe at Play: A Study of Recreation and Leisure Time Activities (New York: A.S. Barnes and Co., 1937), p. 136.
33. Breitmeyer and Hoffman, Sport und Staat, p. 35.
34. Joseph Mathews, "The First Harvard-Oxford Boat Race," The New England Quarterly, XXXIII, #1 (March, 1960), p. 82.
35. Ibid., p. 76.
36. Alexander M. Weyand, The Olympic Pagent (New York: MacMillan, 1952), p. 5.
37. Ibid.
38. Watman, History of British Athletics, pp. 17-18.
39. Charles McCloy, The Measurement of Athletic Power (New York: A.S. Barnes, 1932), p. 1.
40. J. Ashley Cooper, "The Olympic Games," The Nineteenth Century, LXIII, #376 (June, 1908), pp. 380-388.
41. Ibid.
42. Lucas, "Baron Pierre de Coubertin," p. 71.
43. Central Committee in Athens, The Olympic Games, B.C. 776-A.D. 1896 (2. vol., Athens: Charles Beck, 1896), II, p. 2.
44. See Coubertin speech in Isabel Burrows, ed., Physical Training (Boston: George H. Ellis, 1890), pp. 112-115.
45. Central Committee in Athens, The Olympic Games, ii, p. 2.

25

46. F.A.M. Webster, The Evolution of the Olympic
Games, 1829 B.C.-1914 A.D. (London: Heath, Cranton, and
Ourseley, 1914), pp. 173-175.
47. Ernest Seilliere, Un Artisan D'Energie
Francais: Baron Pierre de Coubertin (Paris: Henri
Didier, 1971), pp. 26-27.
48. Coubertin speech in Burrows, Physical Training,
pp. 112-115.
49. American Olympic Committee, Xth Olympiad,
Los Angeles, 1932 (Xth Olympic Committee, 1932),
Frontispiece.
50. Henry, An Approved History of the Olympic Games
p. 32.
51. Coubertin, "The Olympic Games of 1896," The
Century Magazine, LIII, #1 (November, 1896), p. 42.
52. Ibid., P. 40.
53. Central Committee in Athens, The Olympic Games,
II, p. 8.

3

The Early Olympiads

A development parallel to those described in the previous chapter provided the final ingredient required to give the Olympic Games a place in international politics. An explosion of leisure time and recreation accompanied the industrial revolution and the accompanying quantum leap in communication and transporation technologies. The urbanization of work concentrated millions of potential spectators into the cities of Europe and the United States, and created conditions necessary for the development of modern sport, an essentially urban phenomenon.

By the end of the nineteenth century not only was everyone at work together, but everyone was at leisure together as well. The Socialist Movement, concerned as it was with all aspects of social life, was the first transnational political network to use mass leisure for political purposes. The German Social Democratic Party (SPD) was a particular pioneer in the organization of sport and leisure-time activity for political constituents. Between 1890-1914, when the SPD emerged from illegality to become the largest party in Germany, its social clubs and athletic outings advertised social philosophy in an atmosphere of relaxation. SPD activities were precursors of both Marxist and Fascist efforts to control collective social life.

Sport, therefore, was "appropriated"[1] by ideological movements from all parts of the political spectrum. The suggestion that it lent itself to predominantly "right wing" political activity is simply inaccurate.[2] If the conservative forces seem to have an older history in political sport it is because these forces were dominant when sport organization was created. Once underway, however, the process of sport organization was molded by succeeding waves of consumers ranging from Theodore Roosevelt and Adolf Hilter to Nikita Khrushchev and Mao Zedong.

From the first, the political content of Olympic sport was in the eye of the beholder. Even though many teams at the 1896 Games were affiliated with clubs rather than states, winners were immediately identified by nationality.[3] The practice of raising the winner's flag began with the first Olympic Games. These facts may seem trivial now, but their institutionalization assured that athletes' political affiliation would be an important part of the Olympic celebration. The idea that the citizenship or nationality of a victor was a major cause of a champion's victory was not long in coming. Sport was so closely tied to politics by 1908 that the Olympic host that year (Great Britain) defined "country" as "any territory having separate representation on the International Olympic Committee or, where no such representation exists, any territory under one and the same sovereign jurisdiction.[4]

Political identification led to state teams, and soon no athlete could compete as an individual, or appear in Olympic events out of national uniform (these rules still apply). However, "Citizenship" and "Nationality" are terms synonymous only in parts of Western Europe and the United States (and this unity shows signs of cracking). Using state teams as units meant that the Olympic system would be a part of Western political culture. Other peoples entering the system would be forced to conform to Western structures even if artificial state boundaries did not reflect the actual borders of ethnic identification.

This problem surfaced earliest in parts of Eastern and Southern Europe under imperial control. Nationalities which found themselves without states recognized the political implications of Olympic membership and sought it as a public demonstration of political legitimacy. Finnish athletes competed in the semi-offical Athens Games of 1906, but were forced to compete under Russian flags in the 1908 Olympics. As part of the Russian Empire Finland was forced to reflect the status quo in political sport. In the Stockholm Games Finland was permitted a separate sign, but its team had to march with the Russians once more. By 1914 it was reported that Finland had been "wiped off the Olympic map."[5]

The Czechs had a stronger claim to participation, based on the strength of the Sokol movement. Bohemia was a founding member of the Olympic Movement, having representatives both on the IOC and in the early Olympic Games. Austria and Hungary, also with separate

Olympic teams,* became aware of the resulting political
implications and in 1912 prevented independent Bohemian
representation in Stockholm[6] However, they were unable
to dismantle the Bohemian Olympic Committee, which would
serve as the nucleus of the sport organizations for
Czechoslovakia after World War I (creating an uncomfortable position for many Slovaks.)

1896

The first Olympic host was an unstable, relatively
new state in search of political legitimacy. Its ongoing struggle for independence and territorial satis-
faction from Turkey is still a factor in international
politi~s. Questions of nationality and citizenship were
of great importance in the Balkans, and both domestic
and international propaganda campaigns accompanied the
award of the Games of First Olympiad to Greece.
The 1896 Olympics were primarily used as a tool for
national unity by a dynasty under domestic pressure.
The "Greek" royal family was actually a Danish
princely house placed on the throne by the European
Powers after the War of Independence. The Olympic
concept provided the opportunity for the dynasty to tie
its fortunes to the glories of ancient Greece, while
the Olympic system provided political celebration of a
team representative of the modern Greek state.
The award was not greeted with universal enthusiasm
in Athens. Prime Minister Trikoupes opposed the idea
because he felt his country was bankrupt--fiscal problems haunted the first Olympics just as they do today.[7]
Crown Prince Constantine used his personal prestige
to counter Trikoupes and save the Games from financial
collapse. He took charge of the Games Organizing
Committee and found private backing for Olympic stadium
construction (after an appeal for public donations
failed).[8]
Once underway the Games became an arena for political appearances by the royal family. Since in the early
Games rulemaking and judging were left to the hosts,
dukes involved themselves as referees and princesses
handed out prizes. If the Crown Prince did not succeed

---

*Austria-Hungary, the "Dual Monarchy," was actually two
countries united under one dynasty. After 1867 each had
its own prime minister and legislature. The only
ministries held in common were Foreign Affairs and War.
No great love existed between the Monarchy's two pillars,
as witness the rather dirty soccer match they played at
the 1912 Olympics.[9]

in making himself popular (as king he would be ousted
after backing the wrong side in World War I--his father-
in-law was German Kaiser Wilhelm II), he did manage to
get his family noticed. National pride was served well
by the victory of a Greek shepherd in the most prestigious of early Olympic events, the marathon run.

The designation of "marathon" as the name of the
climactic Olympic event had significant political
content. It reminded Europe that Greece had saved
Western civilization from an Asian onslaught. Greek
publicists sought to use this image in the context of
continuing strife with Turkey over the Aegean and
Mediterranean islands between them.

In a September 1895 article in Harper's Weekly,
Demitrios Kalopathakes expressed what Greeks hoped the
First Olympiad would provide.10 He began by saluting
the Anglo-Saxon peoples as the athletic race "par
excellence," and drew a connection between them and the
ancient Greeks (via the Philhellenes?).

Kalopathakes contrasted Greece, as a classical
Western civilization, with the spector of Turkish
oppression in the Balkans. He also compared the
traditions of Greece with what he described as more
recent (and less legitimate) claims by Serbs and Bulgars
in Macedonia. Competing national movements were presented in the context of classical ethnic imagery. In
short, the 1896 Olympic Games were the focus of an attempt to present Greece as a barrier against Turks and
Slavs in modern times as it was against the Persians at
Marathon. Turkey sent no team to the 1896 Olympics; in
1898 the two countries went to war over Crete.

Franco-German rivalry also was evident in Athens.
The Germans carried over resentment at their shabby
treatment at the founding Olympic congress to the first
Olympic Games. In 1895 Berlin, while indicating a
general interest in the Games, stated that Germans would
not go to Athens because of Coubertin's attitude in
Paris the year before.11 The IOC soothed German feelings
by adding a German member, thus ensuring participation
by a German team that reportedly remained aloof from the
other athletes. The Germans concentrated on gymnastics--
a sport in line with the Turnvereine tradition.12

THE LEAN YEARS

Greece sought to become the permanent host of the
Olympics. Had this campaign succeeded the Games might
eventually have become a theater of the Greco-Turkish
war in the 1920s, and perhaps for the Cyprus problem.
The official reason why a permanent Greek site was
rejected was that the IOC wanted to revolve the award
among the "large capitals of the world."13 The IOC had

to choose between a "true" Olympics, i.e. one which was
dominated by Greece and its lore, and a truly international Olympics, one which could flourish in the
political system of its day. While Coubertin saluted
the 1896 celebration as the dawn of a new era for
Greece,[14] he remained intent on bringing his creation
home. Greece was also unsuccessful in getting the IOC
to agree to let it host a quadrennial international
competition halfway between Olympic Games (in line with
the ancient system).[15] The IOC would look back on the
idea with much gratitude after the next two Olympiads.

The first problem Coubertin faced was that no one
in Paris cared as much about the Olympic revival as he
did. The 1900 Olympics were not allowed to stand on
their own, but were submerged within that year's
Paris Exposition. Exposition directors were cool to
the Games, but finally agreed to form a committee to
arrange them.[16] Coubertin did not help his cause when
he suggested that a huge replica of Mt. Olympus be
constructed in Paris.[17] The founder of the Olympic
Movement soon found himself ignored; preparations came
under the control of local boxing, tennis, fencing, and
athletic (track and field) federations.

American athletes had won so many medals in 1896
that their countrymen soon became accustomed to reading
about athletic superiority in the newly developing
"sport pages." American sport officials decided the
world should learn how to train the American way, and
the Amateur Athletic Union (AAU) seized on a plan to
build a large athletic club in Paris for that purpose.[18]
Members of the American Olympic Committee (changed to
United States Olympic Committee only later, when other
"Americans" wanted Olympic status equal to the Yankees)
dissuaded their AAU colleagues from such an assault on
French pride in their own physical culture.

More than pride was hurt when the French announced
the Olympic schedule. Bastille Day (July 14) fell on a
Saturday in 1900, and the French planned to start the
Olympic Games the next day. The Americans protested,
however, saying that they refused to play on the Sab-
bath.[19] The French relented, but only postponed the
crisis one week. In order to fit into Exposition plans
the French decided to hold events the following Sunday,
no matter what the Americans thought.[20] Some US
athletes refused to compete; those who did participate
claimed to be fighting for the flag.[21] Nationalism was
apparently the only acceptable excuse for religious
misbehavior.

US athletes dominated the 1900 Olympics even more
thoroughly than the first Olympic Games. The real
competition was between units from Princeton University,

the New York Athletic Club, and the University of
Pennsylvania. Each of the last two won more medals than
any other country.

The American press soon developed a method of
measuring the victories of American athletes. National
counting systems were never "legal" in the Olympic
system, but were a natural reflection of modern political
sport. The New York Times described the 1900 Olympics
as the "World Amateur Championships," and announced that
the United States had won them.[22]

If the 1900 Games were a slight embarrassment, the
1904 Olympics were a dismal failure. They were awarded
to the United States, partly as a favor to Professor
William P. Sloane, a founding IOC member unlike the
present system, the US was awarded the Games before the
exact site for them had been chosen. Buffalo, Chicago,
and St. Louis all expressed interest. Although Chicago
won the competition, St. Louis did not give up hope of
eventual success, particularly when Chicago began to
complain of money problems.

When inadequate financial backing caused Chicago to
become the first city to return an Olympic award,
St. Louis became the second host in a row to hold the
Games in conjunction with a world's fair. The 1904
Louisiana Purchase Exposition proved to be no more
successful a host than its predecessor.

This was not due to lack of interest. In the
United States, at least, the games drew a great deal of
attention. President Roosevelt personally stepped in
to secure the award for St. Louis once Chicago had
given up.[23] He was, perhaps, the first president to
notice that election and Olympic years coincide, and
that mass attention can be focused on whoever involves
himself in a popular sporting event.

The problem was that no one else bothered to come.
Many Europeans claimed that it was too expensive for an
amateur athlete or his federation to pay passage for
Games that were so far away. Since the British and
French sent no team at all it was easy for the US to
dominate these least international of Olympic Games.
Most of the few medals not won by the United States
went to athletes from Latin America.

PRE-WAR RECOVERY

The Olympic idea nearly died for lack of interest.
The French and American celebrations had been side shows
lacking the international interest necessary to the
Games' competitive political structure. The IOC was thus
receptive to Greek appeals that Olympic officials re-
consider their idea for an inter-Olympic sport meet.

The 1906 Athens Games, although never recognized as an "Olympic" Games, nevertheless were the first really international celebration under IOC control. Most of Europe attended, including such sub-state actors as Cyprus, Ireland and, of course, Bohemia. Even Turkey sent a team to Athens, perhaps reflecting the fleeting vitality of the "Young Turk" Movement, or a temporary lull in Greco-Turkish squabbling.

Despite Coubertin's prediction, Greece had not prospered since 1896. It found itself near bankruptcy after losing the war over Crete. The Balkans were officially "on ice," thanks to an agreement between Russia and Austria-Hungary, so little in the way of territorial conquest was available as a distraction from domestic problems.

The 1906 Games served the latter role quite well. People were given a vacation from their difficulties in order to submerge themselves in classical allegory. Observers at the time noted the cathartic effect the Games seemed to have on a country which was mismanaged and unsure of its future.[24]

A second factor in Greek desires for the meet was the cost of maintaining the Olympic stadium, which had been nearly idle since 1896. George Averoff, the same financial "angel" persuaded by Constantine to back the 1896 Olympics, agreed to refurbish the structure for 1906.[25]

This meet was a great success in comparison to the two previous Olympiads due to global attendance and expanded press coverage.[26] Greek Olympic fervor infected the rest of Europe, which seemed to appreciate the choice of Athens as a sport center. Once more the Greeks tried to have the Games given to them permanently; once more they were refused. Coubertin still dominated the Olympic Movement and continued to hope that the rest of the Western World would catch on to his idea. He felt that this was only possible if each state had a chance to be the center of attention. The 1906 Games demonstrated the classical appeal of Olympic mythology, however, and ancient lore was important in the next Olympic award.

Rome, the second classical city, was the original recipient of the 1908 Olympic Games. Italy was the newest of the "great powers" and also the weakest. The Olympic award was part of an Italian campaign to demonstrate its credentials as a major European actor. Rome's preference for show over substance was illustrated by its attempt to host a great power conference to deal with the Balkans, as well as by its interest in the Olympics.

Italy, however, was in nearly as poor financial shape as Greece. In 1906 Mt. Versuvius staged one of its periodic eruptions, causing such devastation that the Olympic Games had to be sacrificed for the sake of the Italian budget.

On such short notice London, where the Games were transferred, really did rather well. In 1907 the IOC held its Congress in the Hague, i.e. in the same city that hosted the international peace conference. 1908 marked the height of host control over the Olympic Games (at least before 1980). The British were told to design the Olympic medals and pick the Olympic judges.[27] At the time the fairness of this system was not in question, but the problems it created at this Olympics led to the institutionalization of the present Olympic power structure.

In the meantime, the British used Olympic publicity to advertise recent changes in their diplomatic orientation. The past few years had witnessed a revolution in British foreign policy. The Boer War experience was similar to America's Vietnam fiasco in that a power at the height of its influence suddenly found itself both locally impotent and universally disliked; London was shocked to find that Europe's other powers openly enjoyed British discomfort. "Splendid isolation" was no longer viable, and Britain searched for allies. In 1902 she found Japan willing to take on Russia in Northeast Asia. In 1904 an arrangement was made with the old French enemy. France, which had been an ally of Russia since 1894, managed to get her two new friends together in a Triple Entente three years later. In 1908 this was still a shaky arrangement. Britain was suspicious of a Russia which seemed temporarily weakened by war and revolution. The Dogger Bank incident (where Russian ships on their way to destruction by Japan had fired on British fishing boats) was not forgotten, and the Bosnian test of the Entente was just around the corner.

The Anglo-French relationship was also extremely volatile. As a public demonstration of affection, Britain and France staged a public exposition and athlethic exhibition just before the Olympics.[28] This was an early application of the use of sport as a public display meant to affect public relations. Sport displays can reach a wide audience without ever forcing the states involved to deal with difficult problems between them, problems which could mar more traditional diplomatic exchanges.

While this was going on the United States was training its first "national" team. Although national identification already overshadowed club affiliation, the 1908 team was the first chosen after a series of competitive national trials.[29] It would also be the first to "lose" an Olympic Games.

Trouble started early in London. On the opening
day someone forgot to display the Swedish, Finnish, and
American flags in the exhibit to carrying the standards
of the other Olympic participants. Some Swedes picked
up and left. This was embarrassing since they were to
be the next Olympic hosts.[30]

Finland was angry, but could do little about it.
Olympic participation was one of its few international
rallying points, and without a state Finland could do
little in Olympic politics. The Finns stayed in London.

For the US this was a cause celebre. In retalia-
tion Ralph Rose, shotputter and American standard-bearer,
refused to dip the flag in customary courtesy as he
passed Edward VII in the Olympic opening ceremony.
Supposedly he said, "This flag dips to no earthly king."
This phrase--apocryphal or not--demonstrated something of
the revolutionary ideology still preached by the United
States. The perennial Olympic champion perceived itself
to be a young and growing power, rising in strength based
on a new system of government. When American athletes
fresh from the farms or factories defeated European
aristocrats with nothing to do except organize their own
leisure, the lesson learned was that the new world was
rising at the expense of the old.

For the record, the British denied any mischievious
intent, blaming the incident on an incompetent workman.
The Americans were not mollified, and charges flew back
and forth across the Atlantic even after the Olympics
were over.[31] The US has not dipped its flag in any
subsequent Olympic opening ceremony.

American complaints grew louder as the competition
progressed. British judges and organizers were a
pervasive presence, often urging on their athletes as
well as organizing events. On the other hand, American
Olympic Committee officials complained that they were
never allowed near the competition, thus finding it hard
to counter the "home field advantage."[32]

In the 400 meter dash two runners, Halswelle (Great
Britain) and Carpenter (United States) collided. The US
claimed that the British runner tired in the stretch
and fouled his charging opponent. British officials
disagreed, disqualifying Carpenter and declaring "no
race."[33] Belgian observers were quoted by the English
as supporting their position.[34] The Americans refused
a re-race and blasted what they considered to be poor
sportsmanship. The real problem was that the race was
not run in lanes; it was difficult to tell who had fouled
whom.[35]

An even more famous flap came in the marathon. The
first man into the stadium after 26 miles was an Italian
named Dorando Pietri. He was so exhausted that he
collapsed and had to be helped across the finish line.

The British ran up the Italian flag. He had to be
disqualified, of course, placing an American runner
first. American officials claimed that the British had
helped Pietri in order to prevent an American gold
medal,[36] and were displeased when the Italian received a
special gold cup from the British royal family. Interestingly, while photographs and films of the event show
Pietri being helped across the line, the painting
commissioned to immortalize the event made it look as if
he made it on his own.[37]

Anglo-American recriminations continued once the
Games were over.[38] Besides charging that the hosts
cheated during events American Olympic officials claimed
that draws for preliminary heats were fixed by using
green strips for British athletes and white strips for
everyone else.[39]

The bottom line was that the US had been beaten;
the British scored more points. London was enthusiastic,
although the reaction might have been more restrained
had the Organizing Committee told the public how much
the Games had cost. While not admitting any difficulty,
the British Olympic Association made a public appeal for
funds (getting very few).[40]

Questions concerning sub-state Olympic participation
also cropped up in 1908. Although sport representation
does not always mean political independence, separate
status for India and South Africa before a British
Olympic audience in 1908 confirmed the change in
relations within the British Empire. South Africa in
particular used sport for political demonstration since
the South African population was (and is) among the
most sport-conscious in the world.

The United States gave just the opposite message
to Hawaii. Duke Kahanamoku, the great swimmer, was made
an integral member of the American team in each of his
Olympic appearances. By doing so Hawaii was denied what
Puerto Rico would later get, a separate Olympic team
that might serve to rally advocates of political independence.

Coubertin was not pleased with the London show. He
found British preparations overly expensive and conducive
to a carnival atmosphere.[41] By calling for simple
Olympiads with more stress on athletic dignity[42]
Coubertin satisfied his sense of "Olympism," but made no
change in the political and economic future of the
Games. Success bred the kind of spectacle Coubertin
hated because it was precisely the kind of political
event people and governments wanted.

The 1912 Stockholm Olympics went even farther in
this direction, advertising the usual political problems
through the most extensive press coverage of the early
Games. An official film was commissioned to record the

2541 athletes from 28 countries competing in 14 sports.
Preparations were still under host control, but this was
less of a problem since the Swedes were not in a position
to "win" the Olympics.[43]

After losing in London the United States once more
dominated the 1912 Olympics. The US team had a large
military contingent, including a fencer named George S.
Patton.[44] The team's success was attributed to
excellent facilities and good training procedures. In
1912 it was the turn of the British to be jealous,
complaining about "luxurious social clubs" that bank-
rolled American "amateurs." While Americans were proud
to defeat European aristocrats, some Europeans resented
losing to American plutocrats.[45]

The US triumph, however, was marred by the case of
Jim Thorpe. His background and story do not have to be
repeated here, but what is of some political interest is
the mechanism by which he was stripped of his medals.
Once he admitted taking payment for playing baseball he
lost control of his case to the AAU. The latter, as
well as the American Olympic Committee, issued a formal
apology and insisted he return his awards. Sport
organizations tried to excuse his action on his race.
Since he was an Indian, they argued, he did not understand the ways of anyone except "his own people."[46]

Many in the US saw Thorpe's problem as an opportunity for foreigners who were jealous of American sport
to point a finger at its moral deficiencies. A New York
Times editorial put it rather harshly:

> His own disgrace, though lamentable enough, is a
> trivial matter in comparison with the humiliation
> which he has brought upon his country - with
> the derision and denounciation which all Americans
> will have to bear from foreign critics who are
> sure to make the most of the chance given them
> for saying that with us sport is a business and
> that we lack the instinct of fair play.[47]

The Times did praise Thorpe for his honesty in admitting
his transgression, saying this would "set up right in the
eyes of the World."[48]

American sensitivity to foreign reaction was in fact
unnecessary. Although a few British newspapers did see
something typically American in Thorpe's behavior, most
paid little attention to the incident. Some even
expressed sympathy for Thorpe. The Daily Mirror (London)
suggested that others (not just Americans) were under
similar suspicion.[49] More important to the American
Olympic Committee, the consensus seemed to be that
American sport organization was guiltless in the affair.

The Swedes were a little confused. In those days the medals had to be returned to the Olympic host, rather than to any international body. J. Sigfrid Edstrom, Swedish Olympic Committee head and later IOC President, at first refused to take Jim Thorpe's medals back.[50] Edstrom felt that Thorpe's loss of amateur status was punishment enough. Only persistant AAU pressure forced the Swedes to change their minds--after three weeks of consideration.[51]

The Europeans were more impressed with American training methods than with the Thorpe affair. Sir Arthur Conan-Doyle, active in the 1908 and 1912 British efforts, lamented the relatively poor British showing in Stockholm, blaming it on, among other things, a lack of national will. He argued that, since other countries used the Games for political purposes, the British could not lag behind. In order to demonstrate British strength in political sport, Conan Doyle asked for 100,000 pounds to be raised for the 1916 British team through national appeal.[53] Other Englishmen expressed disgust with the Olympics, one suggesting that the British win the Berlin Olympics, and then quit the movement.[54]

There was little likelihood of a 1914 inter-Olympic meet, although the idea of repeating the success of 1906 was suggested following the Stockholm Olympics.[55] Greece once more pressed for a return to Athens, but had to drop this bid when the Balkan Wars gave the dynasty an opportunity for more direct political gains.

Germany, meanwhile, had been a far more eager competitor at the 1908 and 1912 Games than previously. The Germans were pleased with the London show and put in a bid for the 1912 award.[56] German organizers deferred to Stockholm in exchange for 1916, since they calculated that there was no way they could prepare the extravaganza they had in mind in so short a time.[57]

The Berlin Olympics were to have been at Grunewald, near the area chosen for the 1936 Olympics. The Germans planned for an even larger show than Stockholm, but ran into the kind of fiscal problems chronic during Olympic preparation. The Reischstag at first voted down $150,000 in Olympic appropriations as a result of a coalition between Center (Catholic) and SPD deputies. The former were largely from South and West Germany, and refused to sanction an event held for the benefit of Prussia, while the latter claimed that the government favored "better class" athletic clubs over workers involved in SPD sport.[58] The money finally was granted when the Center was persuaded to change its mind.

The issue turned out to be irrelevent. The Olympic Movement was only one of many social movements competing for the loyalty of the world's youth. In 1914 they succumbed to the most direct form of national appeal, marching enthusiastically off to war. The Berlin Olympic Games had to be cancelled, although the VIth Olympiad was still counted in Olympic records.

GROWING PAINS

The success of the last pre-war Olympiads created significant administrative problems which required changes in Olympic organization--changes which further institutionalized the political content of international sport.

The amateur "rule" proved to be especially difficult to enforce, or even define. Coubertin's original intention to restrict Olympic participation to "amateurs" immediately ran up against the military content of national Olympic teams. He therefore exempted officers who fenced from the "amateur" restriction.[59] The IOC still has not reconciled its principles to the Olympic presence of military personnel taking part in "amateur" shooting competition.

The problem of money was more difficult to ignore than that of military amateurs. Sport became successful because of its popular following, and that following began to offer considerable sums to athletes for purposes ranging from professional sport to public relations. The IOC did not attempt to resist this trend. The 1905 Brussels IOC Congress stipulated, for the first time, that "amateurs" could have "out of pocket" expenses reimbursed.[60] Although no other money was allowed to change hands, gifts of products or athletic equipment soon became a gray area. No athlete was supposed to advertise any product, but many did nevertheless.

This issue was further complicated by the fact that there was no single definition of "amateur." Each federation defined the term as it wished, a practice necessary to gain federation allegiance to the Olympic system. The anarchy became institutionalized as the federations got stronger. There has never been a definition of amateur acceptable to every sport organization. With the gradual increase in permissible ways for amateurs to turn a profit, the term became almost meaningless. Still, after the Thorpe incident, Coubertin insisted that future Olympic athletes take an amateur oath during the opening Olympic ceremony. The single thread holding the system together was the rule that an amateur in one sport had to be an amateur in all sports if he or she was to compete in the Olympic Games.

Other problems still plaguing Olympic celebrations originated with the first Olympiads. The winner of the 1904 marathon was disqualified for riding part way in a car. Thomas Hicks, who was then declared the winner,

turned out to have run the race on strychnine.[61] Drugs
could not be tested for with 1904 technology; many
believe they are widely used despite 1980 technology.
    Judging is another old issue. Contemporary viewers
are accustomed to watching political judging. Officials
have always been as likely to rule on a national basis
as on a sporting one in any sport decided by judgment
instead of time or distance. In the 1906 Athens Games
the fencing jury was made up of masters whose students
were the competitors. Judgment was made to protect
teachers' reputations rather than to reward pupils'
skills.[62] Diving judges were also noted for uneven
decisions in the early Games. Before World War I the
problem was compounded by the fact that each national
federation had slightly different scoring standards.[63]
    Perceptions of these problems led to changes in
Olympic organization. Professor Sloane in particular
worried that future Olympics could be wrecked by public
spectacles of cheating and poor judging. After the 1912
Olympics he urged that the 1914 Paris IOC Congress assign
jurisdiction for judging and rulemaking to the individual
sport federations.[64] This was done, and since then the
IOC has seen its authority gradually slip away. With
federations in charge of each sport, and national
Olympic committees in total control over team selection,
the IOC has found itself with little to do besides
selecting Olympic sites, supervising their preparation,
and issuing proclamations concerning the Olympic idea.
As the reality of political sport threatened to make the
last function irrelevent, the IOC felt compelled to
redouble efforts to have its mythology believed. Present
Olympic dogma is not simply an anachronism, it is a
polemical necessity if the IOC is to survive. IOC
resistance to assigning a permanent Olympic site is due
partly to its need to protect the few prerogatives it has
left. Sloane, for his part, recognized that the politics
of sport was not going to vanish, and defended the
significant power delegated to Olympic hosts* in a comment relating to the Stockholm organization:

    This system (host control) has worked fairly well,
    and it would be rather utopian to suppose that a
    people taxing itself to the extent of half a

---

*Cross-cultural problems occured as a result of this,
even when the Olympics were thoroughly Western in participation. The rules for the 1908 Tug-of-War stated that
"regular" shoes should be worn. For the British team,
made up of police, this meant heavy boots.[65] They easily
defeated an American squad in walking shoes, providing
another source of Anglo-American friction.

40

million dollars for building a stadium, creating
an administration, entertaining its guests, and
for all incidentals besides, should forego any
advantage for its contestants by the complete
surrender of itself and its athletic ways.66

The immediate pre-war era did see some interesting
social experiments. ˆ In 1913 the IOC decided to adopt a
"scientific" approach to the creation of better sportsmen, and accepted sport psychology as an Olympic discipline. The original purpose of this was not just to
make better athletes, but to create a "whole physical,
intellectual, moral, and aesthetic way of life.67
Starting with the 1906 inter-Olympics, the
aesthetic aspect of the Games was further encouraged by
the staging of Olympic competition in painting, music,
sculpture, literature, and architecture. These
competitions never attracted the quality of competitors
they were supposed to, and did not have the mass appeal
of sport. Nevertheless, even when the competitions were
ended after World War II, artistic exhibitions continued
in the hope of making the kind of aesthetic statement
Olympic ideologues could be proud of.

NOTES

1.   John Hoberman, "Sport and Political Ideology,"
Journal of Sport and Social Issues, I, 2 (Summer/Fall,
1977), p. 82.
2.   See Ibid, pp. 80-114.
3.   F.A.M. Webster, The Evolution of the Olympic
Games, 1829 B.C.-1914 A.D. (London: Heath, Cranston,
and Ourseley, 1914), pp. 249-250.
4.   British Olympic Council, The Fourth Olympiad
(British Olympic Association; 1908), p. 29.
5.   New York Times, June 7, 1914.
6.   Bill Henry, An Approved History of the Olympic
Games (London: G.P. Putman's Sons, 1948), p. 115
7.   John Lucas, Baron Pierre de Coubertin, p. 114.
8.   Central Committee in Athens, The Olympic Games,
I, p. 19-20.
9.   Swedish Olympic Committe, The Olympic Games of
Stockholm, 1912 (Stockholm, 1913), p. 499.
10.   D. Kalopothakes, "The New Olympic Games,"
Harper's Weekly, XXXIX (September, 1895), pp. 919-124.
11.   Henry, An Approved History of the Olympic
Games, p. 41.
12.   Richard D. Mandell, The Nazi Olympics (New
York: MacMillan, 1971), p. 24.
13.   Central Committee in Athens, The Olympic Games,
p. 81.

14. Baron Pierre de Coubertin, "The Olympic Games of 1896," The Century Magazine, LII, #1 (November, 1896), p. 53.

15. Webster, The Evolution of the Olympic Games, p. 183.

16. Coubertin, "The Meeting of the Olympian Games," North American Review, 170 (June, 1900), pp. 806.

17. William O. Johnson, All That Glitters is not Gold: The Olympic Games (New York: G.P. Putnam's Sons, 1972), p. 73.

18. Henry, An Approved History of the Olympic Games, p. 60.

19. New York Times, July 12, 1900.

20. New York Times, July 16, 1900.

21. Alexander M. Weyand, The Olympic Pagent (New York: MacMillan, 1952), pp. 26-27.

22. New York Times, July 23, 1900.

23. Henry, An Approved History of the Olympic Games, p. 69.

24. J.E. Sullivan, The Olympic Games of 1906, Spaulding Athletic Library, XXIII. #273 (July, 1906), pp. 28-29.

25. Henry Roxborough, Canada at the Olympics (Toronto: Ryerson Press, 1969), p. 29.

26. See New York Times, March 10, 1906, April 26, 1906.

27. Webster, The Evolution of the Olympic Games, pp. 204-205.

28. British Olympic Council, The Fourth Olympiad, p. 46.

29. Johnson, All That Glitters is not Gold, p. 128.

30. Ibid.

31. T.A. Cook, The Olympic Games of 1908: A Reply to Certain Criticisms (British Olympic Association, 1908), p. 46.

32. Roxborough, Canada at the Olympics, p. 40.

33. Cook, The Olympic Games of 1908, p. 18.

34. Ibid., p. 32.

35. Watman, History of British Athletics, p. 43.

36. Cook, The Olympic Games of 1908, p. 19.

37. Dr. Ferenc Mejo, The Modern Olympic Games, (Budapest: Pannonius Press, 1956), illustration following p. 412.

38. See Cook, passim.

39. Ibid., p. 51.

40. Webster, The Evolution of the Olympic Games, p. 217.

41. Swedish Olympic Committee, The Olympic Games of Stockholm, 1912, p. 9.

42. Henry, An Approved History of the Olympic Games, p. 115.

42

43. Webster, The Evolution of the Olympic Games, p. 222.

44. J.E. Sullivan, ed., The Olympic Games of 1912 (New York: American Sports Publishing Company, 1912), p. 64.

45. Webster, The Evolution of the Olympic Games, p. 231.

46. New York Times, January 28, 1913.

47. New York Times, January 29, 1913.

48. Ibid.

49. New York Times, January 30, 1913.

50. New York Times, February 3, 1913.

51. New York Times, February 27, 1913.

52. The Times (London), August 30, 1913.

53. The Times (London), August 27, 1913.

54. The Times (London), September 6, 1913.

55. Webster, The Evolution of the Olympic Games, p. 234.

56. Kurt Doerry and Wilhelm Dorr, Das Olympia Buch (Munich: Olympia Verlag, 1927), p. 8.

57. Weyand, The Olympic Pagent, p. 130.

58. New York Times, January 13, 1914.

59. Coubertin, "The Olympic Games of 1896," p. 46.

60. Webster, The Evolution of the Olympic Games, pp. 192-195.

61. Johnson, All That Glitters is not Gold, p. 124.

62. T.A. Cook, The Olympic Games, (London: Archibald Constable & Co. 1908), pp. 97-98.

63. Ibid.

64. William Sloane, "The Olympic Idea," The Century Magazine, LXXXIV (June, 1912), p. 411.

65. Ibid.

66. Olympic Newsletter (IOC Publication), #11 (August, 1968), p. 358.

67. Roxborough, Canada at the Olympics, p. 40.

4

The Rise and Fall of Internationalism

There was some "sport" in World War I. Soldiers used to chase pigs and hares over the fields of northern France sometimes killing them, sometimes not.[1] A lot of shooting was done, of course, at about anything that moved. Military authorities discouraged some pastimes, especially varieties of fishing involving nets, explosives, and hand grenades.[2]

Although the Olympics were suspended, the Far Eastern Games held their inaugural celebration under Olympic auspices in 1915. These were not as well attended at today's Asian Games but they did serve to keep organized sport functioning. The Far Eastern Games were the conscious model of the first Western post-war athletic meet, the 1919 Paris Inter-Allied Games.

This event was conceived in October 1918 when it was clear that the German armies were collapsing.[3] American officers felt that a celebration of armed victors could preserve the comraderie of the wartime experience and send the men home with memories of peaceful competition with their allies.

One immediate problem was forming the teams. Most of male Europe between the ages of 18 and 26 was dead. Only the United States had fresh bodies saved from the war by virtue of short American participation (April 1917-November 1918). It was no surprise that Americans won half of the events (12) and came second in seven others. There were five clear 1-2-3 American sweeps.[4] Track and field was the main sport, although the United States made one of its periodic and futile attempts at getting the world interested in baseball.

Political problems bridged the gap between 1914 and 1919. The British resented US domination of Games preparations and transferred the pre-war Anglo-American rivalry to the Inter-allied Games. The British did not send an official "team," only individuals who competed as they wished.[5]

Czechs had by now claimed possession of their state (and of its Slovaks), and the Inter-allied Games were an early celebration of it. Czech publicists stressed that Austro-Hungarian tyranny had denied them sporting legitimacy before the War, and that enthusiastic Czech sport teams were one manifestation of the freedom brought their people by the common fight. The Bohemian (new Czechoslovak) Olympic Committee could use its political victory to prepare for the 1920 Olympics.

The Serbs were another favored people in Paris, viewed along with the Belgians as the chief victims of Central Power aggression. As with the Slovaks, few people in the West knew of the existence of Croats and Slovenes and other ethnic groups trying to stave off a Serb dominated state, whether it was called "the Kingdom of the Serbs, Croats, and Slovenes," or "Yugoslavia." The Serbs had enough international sympathy in 1919 to order "south Slavdom's" future as they wished. Even though the "Serb-Croat-Slovene" Committee chose the 1919 team, the athletes were referred to as "Serbs."[6] One rival to "Yugoslavia" did recognize the political value of sport. King Nikita of Montenegro showed up at the Games, as at every public function in Paris, but his claims of sovereignty over his tiny kingdom were totally ignored.

When Prince Faisal of the Hejaz (now called "Saudi Arabia" after the family which overthrew Faisal's sometime later) was invited to gather a team, he sent his emissaries not only to the Arabian Peninsula but to Damascus as well.[7] Faisal, a friend of "Lawrence of Arabia," was the British candidate for the Syrian throne and sought to show his authority there in order to press his rather vast claims at the Peace Conference.

Needless to say, no athletes were invited from the defeated powers. The Greek acceptance to the Inter-allied Games expressed a general feeling:

> As in ancient times, the barbarians were excluded from the Games, (sic) it is the same today. In the Games will participate only the soldiers of the nations which fight for right and the Liberty of the World.[8]

The Inter-allied Games received support from the IOC, which was probably grateful to receive any attention at all. The Olympic Movement needed to regroup, but also had to compete with the memories of war and the hopes engendered by the Peace Conference.

INTERNATIONALISM

For the only time in its history, the IOC tried to graft itself on to the surrounding political system. The popularity of international organization which followed World War I caused a subtle change in Olympic mythology. The terminology used to explain the purpose of the Olympic Movement was altered in order to step in line with the prevailing "internationalist" mood. The IOC now went beyond the goal of aiding the moral development of individual athletes and, for the first time, accepted the idea that participants in sport might be representative of the units of international politics. In 1920 an athletic official defined the purpose of international sport in the wake of World War I:

> The reestablishment of the Olympic Games on a basis and under conditions conformable to the needs of modern life would bring together every four years the representatives of all nations, and it is permissible to suppose that these peaceful and courteous contacts would supply the best of internationalism.[9]

States were assumed to be peaceloving, as long as they were part of the victorious coalition which was in the process of creating the League of Nations. Coubertin himself jumped on the bandwagon of Wilsonian (neo-Kantian) ideology in a letter to the President of the first League Assembly, written shortly after the 1920 Antwerp Olympics:

> Mr. President,
> The International Committee for the Olympic Games, whose head office is in Lausanne and under whose auspices the representatives of 35 nations meet together, cannot allow a great international organization like the League of Nations to settle in their neighborhood without conveying to her their respects and best wishes.
> Twenty-six years ago, our committee introduced and applied, as regards sporting activities, the very principles upon which the League was organized and by means of their Olympiads they brought into existence an international collaboration which is getting closer and more effective.
> After the Triumphal celebration of the 7th Olympiad held in Antwerp, you must be personally aware, Mr. President, of the power attained by the Olympic Movement and you know how much it is bringing together the youth of every country...[10]

The decline of the League system would bring an end to this attempt to give the Olympic Movement an important role in the political system surrounding it. The ideology of sport would then return to its concentration on the function of sport in the moral development of the youth of the world.

FROM ANTWERP TO LOS ANGELES

Antwerp had been in the running for the 1920 Olympic Games before the War, when a six year period was first being institutionalized as the time needed for Olympic preparation. A gaudy book, lauding the advantages of Antwerp, complete with pictures of the royal family and government ministers was sent to each IOC member.[11] Amsterdam, the main rival for the award, published its own pamphlet, but it appeared puny in comparison to the publicity put out by the Belgians. As it turned out, the War was the best publicity the Belgians could have had.

Antwerp, like the rest of northwest Europe, was devastated by the War. The armistice did not give the IOC or its prospective Olympic host much time to get ready, but on April 3, 1919 Antwerp announced that the Games would go on as scheduled.[12] The city could not hope to get itself repaired in so short a time. It proved impossible to supply first-class accomodations after four years of bombardment and bloodshed. This fact did not seem to impress the US team, members of which complained loudly about their living conditions.[13]

If it was a poor physical choice it was certainly the perfect political one. Belgium was the symbol of both courage and horror in war. Belgian bravery was a theme of this athletic celebration; the IOC used the emotional content of this Olympic Games as a lever for organizational rejuvination.

This meant, of course, that once more the villains of the piece could not attend. Sir Theodore Cook of the British Olympic Association had tried to oust Germany from the Olympic Movement as early as 1914.[14] There was no question of Central Power participation in Antwerp, as Coubertin explained:

> A difficult problem posed itself - participation of the Central Empires, as they were now known. Few months had passed since the last German soldiers had left Belgian soil and the last guns had been fired. Good sense indicated that German athletes could not participate...the solution was simple, it was that at each Olympic celebration it is the Organizing Committee that, following the formula established and employed since 1896, issues the invitations.[15]

    Note the difference between this system and present
Olympic rules. Now a host must agree to invite every
state recognized by the IOC. This can be circumvented,
as Canada proved with regard to the "Republic of China"
in 1976, but had this rule been in force in 1920 it
would have been interesting to see how the IOC would
have balanced political necessity with Olympic legality
(the latter is almost always sacrificed to the former).
    The Germans understood the point; the Olympic Games
of 1920 were an early indication of the extent to which
states defeated in World War I were to be political
pariahs. This position was made clear by the US 400
meter relay team, in case anyone doubted the purpose of
German exclusion. Its captain annouced not only that
his colleagues and himself had won the event, but that
in breaking a German-held record they were doing the
world a service.[16]
    Along with the Central Powers, Bolshevik Russia was
kept out of the 1920 Olympics. This caused much less
bitterness in Moscow than German exclusion had in
Berlin since Lenin had as little use for bourgeois sport
as with the coalition of Capitalist powers that ran
Imperialism's "League system." For its part, the IOC
aped Western refusal to recognize the Soviet regime,
retaining among its members a Tsarist representative,
Prince Leon Ourousov.[17]
    These prohibitions extended to most individual
sport federations as well as the IOC. Neither Germany
nor the USSR would be able to celebrate Olympic sport
until, by their choice or that of their adversaries,
they obtained a place in the surrounding political
system. In the Russian case--as later with China--the
IOC lagged behind political reality. While most major
powers recognized the Soviet government by 1933, it was
not until after World War II (and after Hitler's
Olympics) that a Soviet team would participate in the
Olympic Games.
    While old members were excluded, new states were
added to political sport. Brazil, Egypt, Portugal,
Spain, and Switzerland were among first-time Olympic
participants in 1920. It is interesting that Switzerland
decided that Olympic participation would not violate its
canons of neutrality--perhaps its is just as interesting
that it took until 1920 for the Swiss to decide this was
the case.
    Popular postwar denounciation of "militarism" led
some federations to decrease military domination of their
sports. It was only in 1920 that the Equestrian
Federation, for example, made an effort to encourage
civilian participation in its events.[18] Although anti-
militarism was riding high, it could not completely

overcome the participation of athletes in uniform,
particularly among those classes combining aristocratic
background with military service. Soviet Olympic
membership, when it finally came, revitalized the military aspect of the Games; the Soviet bloc continues to
provide more regiments of military athletes than its
"imperialistic" competition.

Paris received its second chance to host the Olympics in 1924. Unlike the last time there was a great
deal of French interest in the Games. Olympic popularity finally enabled Coubertin to receive recognition at
home. If the Belgians would not have German athletes in
1920, the French certainly would not encourage enemy
participation in 1924. Austrian athletes, for example,
were prevented from entering a tennis tournament on the
Riviera during the Olympic year.[19]

The Soviet Union was again left out of the celebration by mutual consent, but this time gave sport some
attention. Besides holding their own Proletarian Games,
the Soviets sent a team to a meet sponsored by French
Socialists.[20] Although Soviet sport organs spent most
of the interwar years struggling against Second International sport institutions, the Games of the VIIIth
Olympiad were held during the "United Front" period,
when fraternization with non-Communist leftist parties
was considered acceptable behavior. Sport really was
the perfect outlet for such a situation. The Soviets
could make a public demonstration of unity without
having to compromise--or even discuss--the difficult
issues dividing communists from socialists.

In the Games themselves the American team once more
came out the "winner." The United States sought to have
the IOC officially recognized the national point system
which every four years institutionalized American athletic superiority.[21] The IOC once more rejected this,
as well as a French system along similar lines.

Two notable changes came to the Olympic system
during this period. First, an old idea finally gained
Olympic acceptance. The IOC had stoutly resisted on
classical grounds nordic states' suggestions that winter
events be celebrated in an Olympic context; the ancient
Greeks had not had Winter Olympics. In 1921 it was
agreed that such an event would be tried on an experimental basis. The first Winter Olympics were held at
Chamonix, France in 1924. At the Prague IOC Congress in
1925 it was agreed that the Winter Games would be
celebrated in each Olympic year. At first, the Olympic
host was given the right of first refusal concerning the
Winter Olympics. In a gesture to Olympic purists it was
decided that these events would not be referred to as
"Olympiads."

   The second development, the revolution in female
participation, was an outgrowth of the first. A few
women had been in the 1906 and 1908 events, and a trickle
of female participation was tolerated on an experimental
basis thereafter. It was the Winter Olympics, and
particularly Sonja Henie, that cemented this process.
Henie was the first in a long line of media commodities
sold through Olympic sport. Her grace and sex appeal--
and three straight figure skating gold medals (1924,
1928, 1932)--led to lucrative contracts for Henie and
increased demand for women athletes in general. Still,
not everyone agreed that women should compete in the
Games. The Pope, for example, called for the Italian
team to prohibit female membership.[22]
   The 1924 Olympics were the last held under
Coubertin's presidency. He resigned his IOC position in
favor of Count Henri de Baillet-Latour of Belgium and
the International Modern Pentathalon Federation.
Baillet-Latour continued to preach Olympic ideology, but
lacked Coubertin's zeal and philosophical depth. As a
result, even greater influence was delegated to the
federations. For a time Baillet-Latour held both his
federation and IOC presidencies; he had as much power in
his former position as in the latter.
   Amsterdam had sought the 1912 and 1920 Olympics
only to lose to rivals with better publicity and more
evident political claim to the award. Los Angeles, its
main opposition for the 1928 Olympics, also seemed to
hold these advantages. However, the IOC was wary of
another trip to the United States, and was equally
reluctant to give the home field advantage to the
perennial Olympic winner. In any case, it seemed to be
Amsterdam's turn, and the Dutch received the award.
   Holland, a neutral in World War I, seemed to be the
perfect choice for the first host of a postwar German
Olympic team. The Germans did well in Amsterdam, but
had a difficult public relations experience. In a soccer
match with Uruguay the Germans had the misfortune both
to play rough and lose. A fight broke out on the field
and 40,000 fans rooted against the Germans. Once more
the image of the "hun" was used to describe German international conduct, doing more damage to the German image
than anything since the War. The Uruguayan Minister to
the Netherlands demanded an apology from the Dutch
Foreign Ministry.[23] The incident could not have done
German-Dutch relations any good.
   Germany had won the 1908 and 1912 Olympic diving
championship, while the United States had been victorious
in 1920 and 1924. The 1928 competition was won by the
Americans, "once and for all (disposing) of the claim
of German superiority."[24]

It was the French team, however, which was involved
in the incident most closely followed at the time. One
day, a Dutch guard at the Olympic stadium refused to
allow the French team to enter for practice. There was
an argument and then a scuffle in which the guard was
knocked down.[25] The French refused to reenter the Games
until the individual was fired.

The American team was led by Douglas MacArthur,
military personality and American Olympic Committee
official. He saw the Games as a measure of the "relative
standing of the nations,"[26]and insisted that the
American point system be used. The IOC refused, but the
American team used it anyway.

MacArthur refused to allow his track and field
athletes to leave their quarters--a ship called the
"President Roosevelt"--except to compete. He was
certain that Europeans were spying on the American team.
Despite (or because of) these precautions the Americans
lost a disappointingly large number of track and field
events (although still "winning" the Olympics overall),
causing the London Daily News to harp on an old theme:

> We own to taking a little quiet satisfaction in
> the surprise expressed in American newspapers that
> the great $500,000 specially trained American team
> should have gone down before British athletes who
> went to Amsterdam in their casual way, fresh from
> their occupations...[27]

There were so many problems in 1928 that the London Times
suggested half-seriously that "the peace of the world is
too precious to justify any risk of its being sacrificed
on the alter of international sport."[28]

Between 1928 and 1932 the IOC tried to wrestle once
more with the amateur issue. The main problem was
"broken time," or the amount of money lost to an athlete
through his or her leaving a job to compete in sport.
Each federation had a different standard for such compen-
sation. In 1930 the IOC reconfirmed that for this concept, as for others under the "amateur" rubric, an
"amateur" in one sport had to be an "amateur" in all
sports.[29] The IOC seemed to have as much trouble with
the word "amateur" as the League had with "aggression" in
terms of deciding just what one was.

1932 was an American show. Lake Placid used the
winter award to become a major resort area, as the Games
were buttressed by CBS and NBC radio coverage. It should
be noted that the area sought a second award immediately
after the 1932 Winter Olympics were over, succeeding
finally for 1980. The recent Lake Placid Olympics was
the vehicle by which the American government subsidized
the retooling of Lake Placid's resort business with over
$50 million in aid.

The summer Games were a Hollywood extravaganza. Los Angeles put on a lavish tenth Olympic Games and thus provided an impressive diversion from the depression. Most of the construction had actually been completed in the 1920's since city fathers had expected to host the Olympics long before 1932. Los Angeles became one of the few cities to complete Olympic construction before the Olympic opening ceremony. The Los Angeles Colosseum was one of the structures originally built for the Games.

The major international political issue dealt with events in China. The Japanese invasion of Manchuria was just a year old, and Japan was still engaged in setting up a puppet "Manchukuo" regime under a member of China's last dynastic family (this move contained an element of logic, since that house had been of Manchurian origin). By trying to get "Manchukuo" into the 1932 Olympic Games Japan provided the United States with its only chance for application of the Stimson Doctrine--the policy by which this country limited its reaction to aggression to a refusal to recognize its political offspring. The Olympic Organizing Committee, backed by the IOC, refused to allow the puppet government to send a team.

This was a textbook example of the political use of international sport. There was no chance that Japan would use the incident as a pretext to go to war with the United States, thus allowing the latter to make a public demonstration of policy without having to back its move with a show of military force. China got the message of the Japanese move, and belatedly sent its own Olympic team to Los Angeles.[30]

President Hoover passed up the opportunity to open the 1932 Games in order to concentrate on his bid for reelection. Considering what happened to him, he probably could have used the publicity.

WEIMAR'S AWARD AND HITLER'S OLYMPICS

For the first few years after the war, Germany had sport relations only with formerly allied and neutral states. The Germans played soccer with Switzerland, Austria, and Hungary as early as 1923; by 1933 contacts were also resumed with the Finns and Dutch.[31]

The first contacts with athletes of an Entente power came through a soccer match with Italy in 1923. Italy was no longer really a member of the enemy coalition. It had been disappointed by Woodrow Wilson's treatment of its claims at Versailles, and under Mussolini had become frankly revisionist. It was not surprising that Italian sporting groups soon established relations with Austria and Hungary, as well as Germany.

The first sport federation to allow Germany back in its fold was the International Fencing Federation. This body even managed to beat the diplomats by a month; Germany was readmitted in September 1925.[32] Italy, long a power in fencing, was instrumental in getting German membership approved.

The statesmen came next, signing the Locarno treaties in October. France, Germany, and Belgium agreed to recognize and maintain their postwar frontiers. Britain and Italy guaranteed the settlement (there was never an "Eastern Locarno," Germany's eastern borders were left conspicuously open to revision). Germany was soon allowed back into the international community, joining the League of Nations in 1926.

Predictably, the Germans then returned to the sporting world with a rush. Soccer relations with France were restored in 1926, the same year as soccer and track and field exchanges were resumed with the British.[33] German crews rowed in the 1926 World Championships.

Germany finally returned to the Olympic Games in 1928, with the mixed results noted above. In 1930 the IOC held its Congress in Berlin, clearly favoring Berlin in its competition with Barcelona for the 1936 Olympic award. The award was finalized two years later.

The parallel between the diplomatic and sporting environments was, in this case, nearly exact. There was little direct state involvement in the process which first banned and then welcomed German athletic participation. Representative sport organizations made the natural connection between sport and politics and acted accordingly. It was easier for the IOC to reverse policy on Germany than, for example, on South Africa in the 1960s. When dealing with Germany Olympic officials acted in accordance with the status quo, while the effort to oust Pretoria went against the policies of those states in control of Olympic politics.

The 1930-1932 award of the Olympics to Germany was simply another expression of the prevailing political environment. It is often forgotten that the Games were awarded to the German Republic, not Hitler's Reich. Weimar hoped to use the Games as a festival celebrating a general German return to respectability. The goals of those awarded the 1936 Olympics were thus remarkably similar to those of the Munich planners in 1972. Both visions were shattered by issues relating to Jewish politics.

Unlike the Munich murders, the perversion of the 1936 Olympics was part of official German policy. While Himmler originally opposed hosting the Olympics, and Julius Streicher called the Games an "infamous" Olympic Game spectacle dominated by Jews, Propaganda Minister

Goebbels recognized the opportunities posed by Olympic politics,[34] and gained Hitler's approval for an altered version of Weimar's award.[35]

The 1936 Olympic Games were used as an appeal to German Volk consciousness, somewhat in the tradition of Father Jahn and the Turnvereine. Beyond this, however, sport was put under the control of a Reichssportfuhrer as it became a tool in the "coordination" (Gleichshaltung) of all aspects of social life (the ability to do that is what separates a modern totalitarian regime from a traditional autocracy). Nazi preparations demonstrated the effectiveness of an athletic appeal to a ruling ethnic group designed to tie toghether concepts of nation, state, and race.

Jews were not viewed as part of this process and were excluded from active participation in Olympic preparations. While the German government did delay application of the most virulent anti-Jewish laws in order to quell threats of an Olympic boycott,[36] internal pressure on Jews continued throughout the period before the Games. Jews were forbidden from displaying German colors if they wanted to celebrate the Olympics; many flew the Olympic flag instead.[37]

While German Jews tried to show loyalty to the Reich, their troubles prompted a significant boycott movement in the United States. Nazi policies combined with prevailing East European anti-semitism to drive many in the East European Jewish cultural and economic elite to the US. America was already a center of Jewish life, but now it became the headquarters of the movement directed against Hitler and toward the creation of a Jewish state in the Middle East. The campaign to prevent American participation in the 1936 Olympic Games was an early manifestation of Jewish political organization in contemporary American politics.

At the end of May, 1933 the American Jewish Committee decided to call for the boycott.[38] In November the AAU came out in favor of that position, threatening to keep its athletes out of Berlin unless Germany changed its policies toward its Jews.[39]

The boycott movement failed because of the personal intervention of newly elected AAU President Avery Brundage and the pressure of German-Americans, who had considerable political leverage of their own. Brundage believed the AAU position amounted to a capitulation of sport to "politics." Brundage went to Germany and received assurances that Jews would be allowed to compete on German teams (Rudi Ball, an ice hockey player, and Helene Mayer, a fencer with one Jewish parent did indeed compete in 1936 as German Olympic athletes). For Brundage this was the key issue. As long as Olympic officials' statements did not reflect government political

policy he felt that Olympic requirements were satisfied.
Since sport and "politics" should be separate Olympic
concern (and jurisdiction) should not extend to political
matters. Brundage came home, declared he found German
Jews satisfied with their treatment, and urged that the
AAU reverse it decision.

This was done, and Brundage was able to assert that
"politics" had been expunged from something above
"politics." He viewed International sport as being
aloof from the political strife of the day. This attitude was reinforced and popularized as Brundage rose
through IOC ranks to become its president from 1952-
1972.

Though crippled, the boycott movement kept active
even after the AAU decision. The NAACP supported the
Jewish effort, but had no effective influence over black
athletes going to Berlin. Violent German pogroms in
1935 briefly caught congressional attention, forcing
Brundage to make a series of public addresses extolling
German preparations and the Olympic ideal. When the
Games were over, Avery Brundage addressed a German-
American day rally in Madison Square Garden and expressed
his gratitude for an American presence in Berlin:

> We can learn much from Germany. We too, if we
> are to preserve our institutions, must stamp out
> Communism...Germany has progressed as a nation out
> of her discouragement of five years ago into a
> spirit of confidence in herself...No country since
> ancient Greece has displayed a more truly national
> interest in the Olympic spirit than you find in
> Germany today.[40]

Brundage went on to thank his audience for opposing the
"small but highly financed" minority who had tried to
prevent American participation in the 1936 celebration.

IOC President Baillet-Latour was more disturbed by
Hitler's intentions than Brundage, at least to the extent
that he insisted on German recognition of IOC authority
over the Olympics and the Olympic site during the Games.
He told the Führer that the Olympics were always held in
ancient Olympia, no matter what city they appeared to be
in.[41]

A certain Bruno Makitz agreed that there was something un-German in Olympic preparations:

> Frenchmen, Belgians, Polacks, and Jew-niggers run
> on German tracks and swim in German pools. Good
> money is thrown away and nobody can truthfully say
> that international relationships between Germany
> and its enemies have been bettered. Only a few
> treasonable persons and anti-German pacifists claim

> such accomplishments when speaking in Geneva,
> Paris, and Prague. As a matter of fact we consider
> them (the Olympics) necessary due to international
> propaganda. The difference with us will be that no
> private clubs or associations will name the teams
> in the name of Germany and put Germany to shame.
> The state will name the teams.[42]

Meanwhile, during the Olympics, Spanish athletes had to
be protected, since their non-Nordic features led them
to be mistaken as Jews, and treated accordingly.[43]

In the end, although the Netherlands and others
considered a boycott only Ireland stayed away from
Berlin. The British position was typified by Lord
Aberdeen, who reasoned that Britain should have no prob-
lem attending the Berlin Olympics, since it had so few
Jewish citizens.[44]

Hitler's Games proceeded smoothly. The Winter
Olympics, held at Garmisch-Partenkirchen, were a great
help to the German image.[45] Hitler was aware that many
were watching for a hint of German policy toward the
summer show, so he kept the presence of Party ideologues
and military uniforms at a minimum. The US boycott movement finally died after the success of the Winter
Olympics.

In March, as preparations continued in Berlin,
Hitler remilitarized the Rhineland. This time some in
France did suggest a boycott and the Chamber of Deputies
refused to subsidize team travel to Berlin. Private
organizations, however, were allowed to take up the
slack. In the opening Olympic ceremony the French team
gave Hitler the Olympic salute--a straight extension of
the right arm. Germans fans mistook it for the Naxi
salute and perceived the appropriate political message,
giving the French a standing ovation (see Leni
Riefenstahl's film of the Games). At the same time the
British Permanent Undersecretary for Foreign Affairs,
Sir Robert Vansittart, visited Berlin and stressed that
Anglo-German relations were friendly, the Rhineland not-
withstanding.[46] For his part, Baillet-Latour saw no
problem with the German move,[47] allowing the Germans to
proceed as if nothing had happened.[48]

Despite Jesse Owens' efforts Germany "won" the 1936
Olympic Games. In addition, German delight at the presence of so many superior physical specimens led to an
unusual Olympic experiment. The Reich hired German girls
to become pregnant by the athletes in order to introduce
superior genes to the race.[49] The women were promised
that the state would care for the children once they were
born. Hitler enjoyed his Olympic Games, telling Albert
Speer that following the Tokyo Olympics in 1940 Germany
would forever be the Olympic host.[50]

The 1936 Olympic Games were the most lavish yet held. They clearly overshadowed rival Games which were meant to provide a progressive alternative to the Nazi show. The main center of these efforts was Barcelona (Tel Aviv and Prague were two others), which was not only Berlin's main competitor for the 1936 award, but also a center of Spanish radicalism. Athletics had to compete with the Spanish Civil War, however, and came in a poor second.

INTERRUPTIONS AGAIN

Baron Pierre de Coubertin died on September 2, 1937. He was buried at IOC headquarters in Lausanne--except for his heart, which was transported to Olympia.

Preparations for 1940, meanwhile, were dominated by the Tokyo-Helsinki competition for the summer Olympic Games. Baillet-Latour visited both cities, praising both on their Olympic spirit and showing little in the way of favoritism.[51]

Berlin viewed Tokyo's eventual success as evidence of the resurrection of the Anglo-Japanese alliance.[52] London and Rome had both made half-hearted bids for the twelfth Olympic Games. The fact that London withdrew in order to obtain the 1944 award made less of an impression on Germany than the fact that Japan was the immediate beneficiary of that British decision.

Japan did not hold the award long. In 1937 the Sino-Japanese "incident"--an invasion of northern China by Japanese armies--demonstrated that Japan was committed to a major war in Asia. Under such circumstances they returned the Games to the IOC, which then conferred them on Helsinki. Japan held an all-Japan meet instead, and later planned events including the areas under the jurisdiction of the Greater East Asia Co-Prosperity Sphere.

Finland had been interested in being an Olympic host since the successful Stockholm Games turned world attention on Finland's main sport rival (the two countries broke off sport contacts for a time in the 1930s). The Finns also remembered the effect of political sport on their drive for recognition before World War I.

Under these conditions the invasion of Poland did not stop Finnish preparations for the 1940 celebration, and neither did the outbreak of war between Finland and the Soviet Union two months later (November, 1939). As late as February 1940 the Finnish Olympic Committee was printing tickets to Olympic events and expressing hope that the athletes of the world would gather for the Olympics as a sign of opposition to Soviet aggression.[53] Logistics regarding the relay-team of athletes carrying the Olympic flame from Olympia to Helsinki were finally in March, but by April it was clear that they would not be able to make the run. Germany had invaded the Low Countries, France would be next, followed by Yugoslavia, Greece, and the USSR. While Germany held an athletic meet attended by athletes from such states as Croatia and Slovakia (representing ethnic groups ignored in 1919), the Olympic Movement waited for another war to end.

NOTES

1.   Anthony Buxton, Sport in Peace and War (London: Arthur L. Humphreys, 1920), pp. 48-49.
2.   Ibid., p. 1.
3.   Games Committee, The Inter-allied Games of 1919 (Paris; Publications Periodiques, 1919), p. 14.
4.   Ibid., p. 177.
5.   Ibid., p. 171.
6.   Ibid., p. 98.
7.   Ibid., p. 56.
8.   Ibid., p. 55.
9.   American Olympic Committee (AOC), Report of the AOC, VII Games, 1920 (AOC, 1920), p. 78.
10. Journal of the First League Assembly, #8 (November 23, 1920), p. 67.
11. IOC, Aurons-Nous La VIII Olympiade a Anvers en 1920? (Antwerp, 1920).
12. AOC, Report of the AOC, 1920, p. 7.
13. Ibid., p. 33.
14. Heinz Harder, Unternehmen Olympia (Cologne: Kiepenheuer und Witsch, 1970), p. 78.
15. Henry, An Approved History of the Olympic Games, p. 135.
16. AOC, Report...1920, p. 231.
17. Ibid., pp. 429-430.
18. Ibid., p. 451.
19. New York Times, April 25, 1924.
20. New York Times, May 11, 1924.
21. New York Times, June 24, 1924.
22. Florence A. Somer, Principles of Women's Athletics (New York: A.S. Barnes & Co. 1928), p. 55.
23. Roxborough, Canada at the Olympics, p. 70.
24. AOC, Report of the AOC-1028, St. Moritz and Amsterdam (New York: AOC, 1928), p. 293.
25. John R. Tunis, Sports (New York: John Day Co., 1928), p. 95.
26. AOC, Report-1928, p. 1.
27. Weyand, The Olympic Pagent, p. 191.
28. Roxborough, Canada at the Olympics, p. 71.
29. Henry, An Approved History of the Olympic Games, p. 299.
30. Ibid., p. 211.

58

31. Doerry and Dorr, Das Olympia Buch, p. 92.
32. Ibid., p. 249.
33. Ibid., p. 59.
34. Henry, An Approved History of the Olympic Games, p. 230.
35. New York Times, December 15, 1933.
36. New York Times, December 1, 1935.
37. Weyand, The Olympic Pagent, p. 251.
38. New York Times, May 31, 1933.
39. New York Times, November 21, 1933.
40. New York Times, October 5, 1936.
41. Johnson, All That Glitters is not Gold, p. 23.
42. Irving De Koff, The Role of Governments in the Olympics (Ed.D. dissertation, Columbia University, 1962), p. 47.
43. Judith Holmes, Olympiad 1936 (New York: Ballantine, 1971), p. 24.
44. Holmes, Olympiad 1936, p. 37.
45. Ibid., p. 67.
46. New York Times, August 10, 1936.
47. New York Times, March 11, 1936.
48. Richard Mandell, The Nazi Olympics (New York: MacMillan, 1972), p. 111.
49. Johnson, All That Glitters is not Gold, p. 29.
50. Mandell, The Nazi Olympics, p. 293.
51. New York Times, April 23, 1936, May 6, 1936.
52. New York Times, August 1, 1936.
53. New York Times, February 11, 1940.

5

The Cold War

The end of the Second World War did not result in the "internationalist" optimism of 1919. For one thing, World War II could not have been won without the Soviet Union, a power for which "internationalism" meant something much different than for its allies. Even before the wartime alliance broke up it was clear that the victors did not have the ideological compatibility necessary to create a unified international system.

In addition, the failure of the League cautioned those who created the United Nations organization in 1945 and reminded the IOC that political internationalism was, at best, a fleeting phenomenon. Since politics had failed to accomplish Coubertin's ideals, the Olympic system decided to attempt to accomplish the purpose itself. In 1949, when the Cold War was obviously underway, the IOC set up the International Olympic Academy to steep young people in Olympism.[1] In doing so the IOC tried to ignore the basis for its strength, public attention. Training a few people in Olympic lore could not offset either the close ties between Olympic organization and international politics or the popularity of political sport.

The British undertook their second Olympic award with a little more warning than they had had in 1908. The 1944 Games were merely postponed four years, giving London some time to catch its breath from the War and allowing Helsinki until 1952 to prepare for an Olympiad promised since 1938.

British preparations proceeded on the assumption that an organizing committee should not go into debt, an assumption rarely taken in the years to come. The British Olympic Association had been strained financially by its 1908 planning, and knew that it could not count on any public donation in the wake of wartime devastation The British managed to prepare the 1948 Olympic Games without going to the government or the public for money.

The United States also remembered the last London Games. The squabbles between the two sides had been embarrassing, and if repeated would hurt the campaign to keep Americans interested in their European allies (and responsibilities). In 1948 Olympic official Gustavus T. Kirby, a veteran of the 1908 American Olympic effort, congratulated the British on both sportsmanship and teamwork.[2] The Western democracies put on a show of unity in London while it was being tested in Berlin.

As after World War I, the losers were left out of Olympic sport.* This time the IOC could claim that no legitimate government existed in Germany or Japan to which a national Olympic committee could be accredited. Rather than explicitly keeping out Axis athletes, the IOC insisted that it was waiting for Germany to be reunited before accepting its participation in sport. When political developments created two German governments instead of one, the IOC was faced with a political issue that it dealt with in a manner analyzed later in this chapter.

Japan, at least, remained united (except for Soviet annexation of the Kurile islands in the north and the American occupation of Okinawa in the south). Olympic veteran Douglas MacArthur decided that the Japanese were not ready to reenter international sport in 1948. However, in 1952, in the wake of the Japanese-US peace treaty and security agreement, MacArthur allowed Japan to recreate its national Olympic committee and to compete in the Olympic Games.[3]

Old wounds were quickly overshadowed by new international competition as the Soviet-American rivalry revealed itself. While former great powers became arenas for dispute, former allies became major adversaries.

The Cold War has been fought with a massive commitment of resources by the two most powerful states in the world. Yet the questions of ideology and power that divide them have not been tested in the usual manner; there has been no contest of arms to determine the strongest, the smartest, the society with History on its side.

If these states have not gone to war, neither have they settled their differences. The fact that both have placed restraints on their use of strategic power has not led to any decrease in the intensity of the struggle between them ("Detente" is a process of defining the paramaters of conflict. It has nothing to do with the

---

*Italy switched sides in 1943 and was represented in London. The Italians refused to distribute the 1948 Olympic film, however, because it did not feature any Italian medal winners.

problems which divide the adversaries). They have
competed in any non-strategic way open to them, and
sporting "combat" has been one of these.

The US and USSR use both the public, politically
peripheral nature of sport and the linkage between
physical culture and national defense in their struggle.
Sport is one of the favorite arenas for demonstration
of the relative prowess of the New Soviet Man and All-
American boy. Since the societies of both superpowers
are future oriented, the use of sport on both sides of
the iron curtain reflects the desire of each superpower
to demonstrate superior vitality.

Some organs of the Olympic Movement could only serve
a secondary role in Cold War Soviet-American athletic
relations. The United States was not a member of
regional European sport federations and, therefore,
could not use regional games to establish contacts with
the USSR. Those international federations that held
world championships did not, in first two decades of
the Cold War, attract the public attention necessary for
the full utilization of sport as a tool in public
diplomacy. So the major medium of US-USSR athletic
diplomacy has been bilateral exchanges between the two
sides.[4]

The Olympic Games themselves have served as points
of contact. Although they take place only one in four
years, and thus cannot serve as a forum for regular
exchanges, they do attract more attention than other
events, and therefore involve more prestige as well.

DEFINING RELATIONSHIPS

At first, Soviet sport policy reflected the caution
evident in Stalinist relations with the Capitalist
world. The USSR was not yet sure if the US or Britain
would be its prime adversary. The United States was
the strongest power in the world, but it had held that
distinction in 1919 and yet had chosen to isolate itself
from European politics. Britain, though obviously
weakened by the War, still possessed an empire stocked
with military bases ringing the Soviet Union.

There is evidence that the Soviets were not sure
what their policy would be toward the organs of
international sport in the first years after the war.
The Olympic Movement had ignored Bolshevik Russia before
1945. Moscow apparently did not understand that being
on the winning side in World War II, and emerging from
it the strongest power in Europe, automatically
qualified it for participation in postwar political
sport. Between 1945 and 1952 there was no question of
the IOC barring the Soviets, only whether the USSR
would choose to take part in Olympic activity.

In September 1945--before anyone knew there was
going to be any Cold War--the International Amateur
Athletic Federation (IAAF--the body that runs track and
field) invited Soviet athletes to enter the 1946 European track and field championships. The IAAF may simply
have assumed that the wartime coalition would continue
into the postwar era, and that Soviet athletes would
logically take part in the revitalization of European
sport. In any case, the Soviets sent no reply, but
simply sent a team to Oslo. It was reported that Soviet
athletes pushed themselves around quite forcefully and
showed no inclination to accept federation rules or
jurisdiction.[5] If true, Moscow might have felt no
inclination to respect organs of bourgeois sport as long
as the advance of Socialism to the Atlantic appeared
possible. This Soviet attitude also extended to bilateral exchanges, as reflected in the 1945 tour of
Great Britain by the Dynamo soccer club. Soviet
officials insisted on bringing along their own referee,
openly distrusting all suggestions that local people
be used.[6]

This situation did not extend to the Soviet's new
allies in Eastern Europe. The 1948 Olympics provided
a rare symbol of continuity in Cold War Europe. The
new "People's Democracies" were successors to East
European Olympic committees as well as to pre-war
governments. They all sent teams to the 1948 London
Olympics despite Soviet abstention from most international events.

For Czechoslovakia in particular the 1948 Olympics--
and the exploits of Emil Zatopek--meant more than just
athletic triumph. Czechoslovkia remained heir to the
Sokol tradition and indicated, just before the February
1948 coup against non-Communist elements, that it
would like to retain good sporting relations with the
West (Prague was also the only East European regime to
show interest in the Marshall Plan).

Interest in sport proved as abortive as feelers
for economic assistance. An Anglo-Czechoslovak soccer
match was cancelled in April 1948 as the Czech government announced that its Football Federation no longer
existed.[7] Until this federation was reconstituted
Czechoslovak teams were cut off from non-Communist contacts.

Czechoslovak participation in the Olympics later
that year was probably acceptable to Moscow since by
then the political situation was under control and
because the Czechoslovak team was in the safe company
of the rest of Eastern Europe (even so, several East
bloc athletes defected in 1948, signalling a chronic
problem for Socialist sport).

Yugoslavia was much more of a political headache. The split with Tito had its expression in sport through cancellation of the 1948 Balkan Games. Tito had hoped to create a Balkan Federation under his influence and that of Bulgaria's Georgi Dimitrov. The Balkan Games Committee was created to provide a public demonstration of the new regional balance, but found itself cut adrift by Stalin's expulsion of Tito from international Communism. Yugoslavia reported that Bulgarian and Albanian delegations did not bother to show up at the meeting which was supposed to organize the Games.[8] It should be noted that ideological problems were supplemented by Bulgarian claims to Macedonia and Albanian fears of Yugoslav annexation.

East Europeans who lost their countries also lost sporting identity. Non-Communist athletic refugees from Eastern Europe sought to compete in the 1952 Olympic Games as individuals or, preferably, as the "true" representatives of their former homes. This was politically impossible; the IOC would never permit a separation of athlete and state. In this case the IOC proved a more perfect reflection of reality than regular diplomacy. The United States still maintained the fiction of "Latvia," Lithuania," and "Estonia" by allowing them to retain their Washington embassies. President Ford explicitly excepted the Baltic states from his recognition of the post-1945 territorial status quo as represented by the 1975 Helsinki Accord. No such policy was possible in European sport.

While Germany and Japan attended the 1952 Olso Winter Olympics (Norway worried that there would be anti-German incidents), Moscow did not. As with the 1945 track and field championships the Soviets gave no notice of their position and no reason for it. Similarly, Soviet participation in that year's summer Olympics was questionable until shortly before they were held.

In 1950 the IOC reported that three invitations had been sent to Moscow, none of which had earned a reply.[9] In fact the USSR had been gradually adjusting to the rules and standards of each federation as it joined the Olympic system. In May 1951 the IOC unanimously voted the USSR into its Movement.[10] All the Soviets would say was that they might send a team to the 1952 Olympics, but only if the IOC would satisfy certain conditions.*

---

*For example, until 1952 commissioned officers were the only military personnel allowed in the Olympics.[11] This was changed at Soviet request. The largest influx of military athletes to the Olympics since World War II has come from the Soviet bloc.

Moscow sent observers to the Oslo winter Olympics. Ignoring the Finnish Olympic Committee (the host sends the official invitations), the Soviets waited until July 1952 until announcing through the Finnish Communist Party that they would indeed attend the summer Olympics.[12]

Finland was a logical choice for initial Soviet Olympic participation. Not only was it close to the USSR, but the two countries were in the process of working out an agreement whereby Finland recognized preeminent Soviet interest in its foreign policy (this did not mean that Finland was a Soviet satellite-- "Finlandization" is an overstated concept).

By now the United States had definitely been identified as the prime enemy, and it was to America that both Soviet athletes and propagandists turned their attention. In fact both powers used their first Olympic clash as a conscious crusade against each other.

Soviet bloc athletes remained aloof from other teams. The USSR charged that the United States was one vast military camp and that the Americans were trying to take over international sport as they had international politics.[13] The Soviets later embellished this with the idea that "Olympic" meant "business."[14] The USSR described the Olympic Games as a vast profit-making circus in which Capitalists squeezed money out of people cauterized by phony Olympic ideology.

When the Bulgarian team showed up in Helsinki, Moscow labeled it as the first of the "Peace Camp" to show up at the Olympics.[15] The same week the entire Soviet bloc held a meeting of the "World Federation of Democratic Youth" in Helsinki.[16]

The other side churned out its own propaganda. American publicists claimed that Stalin had established athletic factories in which he trained unfeeling robots who he would unleash at Helsinki.[17] Decathalon champion Bob Mathias described the 1952 Olympics Games in the following way:

> There were many more pressures on American athletes because of the Russians than in 1948. They were in a sense the real enemy. You just loved to beat 'em. You just had to beat 'em. It wasn't like beating some group from a friendly country like Australia (the next Olympic host). This feeling was strong down through the entire team, even in sports where the Russians didn't excel.[18]

In 1952 the Soviet Union challenged the American model of national point tabulation. The USSR derided the American point system as the "General MacArthur" system and denounced it as evidence of imperialism in

American sport. The Soviets instituted their own
system, which put less of a premium on first place and
more on team depth.[19]

Using two different scoring methods each side could
claim victory in 1952. Later the USSR relented, listing
the 1952 Olympics as a tie (while showing how Moscow
"won" each of the next Olympics through 1964).[20] The
1952 Olympic Games were a perfect example of sport
reflecting the prevailing political mood, and the mood
was bad.

This was in marked contrast to the situation four
years later, at least regarding Soviet-American relations. The Melbourne Olympics opened as international
relations were convulsed by the twin crises of Suez and
Budapest. The latter was reflected in the mass defection of the Hungarian Olympic team to the West. Hungary
accomplished some measure of revenge when its water polo
team defeated the Soviet side 4-0 in one of the blood-
iest matches ever played.

The prevailing atmosphere at the Games, however, was
more representative of the cooperative attitude existing
between the superpowers regarding the Suez problem.
Soviet and American policies had in common their desire
to secure British, French, and Israeli withdrawal from
the Suez Canal and Sinai Desert. The Games were also
an accurate reflection of attitudes inherent in a policy
of "Peaceful Coexistence," an offensive strategy
Khrushchev put forward as a way to control the struggle
against Capitalism in an era when the prime adversary
was still too strong to confront in a direct--nuclear--
manner.

Soviet and American athletes were prominently dis-
played in friendly articles, photgraphs, and medal award
ceremonies. In addition, Soviet and American sport
officials engaged in discussions directly affecting
future Soviet-American sport exchanges.[21] The 1956
Olympic Games were the most public forum in which the
new relationship could be introduced. Talks continued
after the Games and were supplemented by government
negotiations resulting in the cultural agreement of
1958. As with "Ping Pong Diplomacy," sport publicity
prepared people for more regular diplomatic relations,
as represented by Khruschev's trip to the US in 1959.

INSTITUTIONALIZED US-SOVIET RIVALRY

The 1958-1966 Soviet American track and field
exchanges were the most popular sporting meets in the
Cold War, and the major athletic fruit of the "Peaceful
Coexistence" era. Track meets drew many fans, commerical
sponsors, and a great deal of television coverage. The
great meets of this period thus received the exposure

necessary for effective public diplomacy. These annual
affairs, hosted alternatively by each side, became a
regular and systematic form of Soviet-American rivalry.
They served to reduce the stereotyped fear of the "Enemy"
as presented to both publics by their respective presses.
Already by 1959 American sportswriters were allowing that
the Soviets could be "ordinary human beings."[22]

This atmosphere was extended by the 1960 winter
Olympics at Squaw Valley, California. The Soviet team
put on a friendly face, mixing with both American
athletes and spectators.[23] In addition, the ten or
twelve IOC votes controlled by the USSR went to Detriot
over Tokyo in the voting for the 1964 Olympic award.
Some felt that the Soviets merely wanted to gain
propaganda points by showing off their athletes before
enemy fans,[24] but it is just as likely that this was a
genuine gesture reflecting the positive aspects of
Soviet-American relations in the era of the second
Berlin crisis.

However, sport also focused public attention on
international relations when they went sour. In the
early 1960's, when Moscow worried over the extent to
which UN Secretary-General Hammerskjold exhibited
independence, the Soviets tried to replace his office
with a "Troika" system of three executives, one from
each bloc and a third agreed to by the superpowers. In
1961-62 Soviet distrust of Olympic officials led Moscow
to try to dilute the IOC in a similar manner. They also
suggested adding to the latter all heads of sport
federations, leading IOC President Brundage to charge
that Moscow was trying to take over the Olympic Movement.[25]

Soviet-American track meets, meanwhile, survived the
U-2 incident, the Second Berlin Crisis, the Cuban Missile
Crisis, and the abrupt changes in both superpower regimes
in 1963-64. However, they finally became a victim of
the American escalation of the air war over Vietnam.

In 1966 the Soviets cancelled the track meet
scheduled for that year in Los Angeles (costing the
Los Angeles Times a great deal of money). A State
Department spokesman offered one possible reason for the
move--"they saw a bad licking staring them in the
face."[26] A more plausible explanation was that which
the USSR itself offered. It cancelled the meet because
of the War. The Soviets were greatly embarrassed by
their ability to halt the American bombing of North
Vietnam. The Soviet leadership was also put on the
defensive by the harsh Chinese reaction to the lack of
apparent Soviet action in the area. The termination of
the major sport institution of the Cold War was the most
public way in which Moscow could demonstrate its opposition to US policy without risking political or military

reprisal. This negative action underscored the limit of a superpower's influence in the contemporary era (something the other superpower was learning at the same time in the same place).

There were other manifestations of this Soviet use of sport. The World University Games of 1966 were a forum for an apparently sullen and uncooperative Soviet team, one which reverted to the Cold War style of 1952. That same summer the Soviets abruptly cancelled a basketball game with an American team, resulting in an official US government protest.

The most blatant use of sport to publicize the depth of feeling over Vietnam came in 1968 at Bulgarian initiative. During preparation for a track meet in Sofia, the government announced that the medals to be awarded would be made out of metal from American planes shot down over Vietnam.[27]

Vietnam was not the only issue the Soviets raised in political sport. In 1968 Yevgeny Yevtushenko took the opportunity to write a poem celebrating John Carlos and Tommie Smith for their protest of American racial policy on the award winners' platform in Mexico.[28] In a way this made up for some of the embarrassment caused by world reaction to the invasion of Czechoslovakia and the call by Emil Zatopek for the expulsion of the Soviets from the 1968 Olympics. The Smith/Carlos episode provided evidence that life in the West was not all it was advertised to be.

The public is by now used to superpower rivalry in international sport. Claims of supremacy are expected and charges of foul play are common. Since there are few political surprises left, since nothing is groundbreaking any more in bi-lateral superpower sport, Soviet-American competition is now interesting simply as political rivalry between well-known adversaries. The track and field exchanges have been resumed, but now are merely part of the pattern of competition expected in political sport.

GERMANY

Meanwhile other issues complicated Cold War sport. More and more, as the Olympic system grew, smaller countries found themselves competing in Olympic politics.

Germany was a focal point for political sport as well as for international politics in general. It was only when Europe was clearly divided into two camps that the allied occupation zones in the former Reich were set up as separate states.

This situation petrified after 1949, presenting unique problems for the Olympic Movement. Legally there was still one Germany; all sides officially agreed that the goal of their policies was eventual reunification. Whatever private desires were held by the leaders of each "Germany," in public each superpower and its clients continued to speak of one German nation. Only under Willy Brandt would the West Germans admit to the existence of two German states. In sporting politics public posture is more immediately relevent than secret diplomacy, so IOC policy continued to be based on the fiction that a united Germany still existed, and that one German team should be chosen for the Olympics.

This public posture gave both sides a way of expressing an interest in unification without having to do anything to bring it about. It is not clear that Konrad Adenauer really wanted to rejoin his state with eastern districts known for their traditional loyalty to the SPD, the main rival to his newly-formed Christian Democratic Union (CDU). For its part, East Germany (the German Democratic Republic--DDR) could use sport to celebrate one Germany, while all the time striving for recognition of its separate status.

Olympic unity served the West better than the East; the Federal Republic was stronger in both economic base and political position. The IOC recognized the West German Olympic committee in 1951. Possessing by far a larger population and more widespread political acceptance, Bonn quickly came to dominate the unified teams celebrating Olympiads from 1952-1964, thus causing the East Germans to demand separate sport representation. Part of the drive toward sporting supremacy now so important to the DDR can be traced to its experience as **a repressed** junior partner in postwar international sport.

In May 1951 representatives of the two Germanies agreed to form a single Olympic team for the 1952 Helsinki Games.[29] When the two sides met in November to discuss details, some noted that this was among the first instances of intra-German contact since the War.[30]

In fact, however, this was simply an opening round in a struggle for legitimacy carried on in Olympic politics. The West Germans dominated national Olympic committee organization, and clearly had the final word in choosing the team. When the East Germans balked at some of the arrangements, the West Germans threatened to cut the DDR off from any participation at all.[31] West Germany clearly was reluctant to share the team in any case, and revoked its threat only after pressure from the IOC and the USSR was not countered by support from the West.

In February 1952 the Germans attempted to hold a "team" meeting. By this time the East Germans had given up any hope of controlling the 1952 team, so concentrated instead on a demand that they be granted a separate Olympic committee recognized alongside the "national" organization so clearly controlled from Bonn.[32] The West Germans naturally opposed any such creation claiming that, since there was only one Germany and since the IOC had already recognized its Olympic committee, there was no need for a new one. The IOC agreed, insisting on both a single organization and Olympic team, at least through Helsinki.

The DDR pressed its case both for a separate Olympic committee and the right of increased jurisdiction in team selection in preparation for the next Olympic Games. The East Germans had just begun to build their awesome sport program so, calculating that they had little chance to win a great number of medals in Melbourne or Cortina d'Ampezza, they concentrated instead on separate organizationally status. In June 1955 they offered to hold talks with the West Germans on selecting the 1956 teams, hoping to get for themselves a larger voice in team selection and, through this, a permanent insititutional presence in German political sport.[33]

Although denied any opening from Bonn, East German policy proved partly successful in international organs. The IOC granted East Germany its own national Olympic committee in 1955 on a provisional basis, but the DDR still could not choose its own Olympic team. This recognition of its separate existence, although limited, was one of the earliest forms of political recognition of the DDR outside the Soviet bloc.

This arrangement required some political gymnastics at the Games themselves. When there was a "unified" team a compromise flag was carried. The five Olympic rings were superimposed on the black-red-gold tricolor which formed the basis for both German flags. In addition, German Olympic victors were saluted to the strains of a Beethoven hymn rather than either national anthem.

The German problem had its manifestations in each federation as well as at the Olympics. Federations have total control over membership policy, so one's policy did not necessarily provide a precedent for the others. The East Germans were able to secure separate representation in some federations in the mid 1950s, while in others they had to wait for many years before being allowed a separate team. Some did not allow a DDR team until it was clear that there would be two German teams at the 1968 Olympic Games.

Any sport could be used as an example of the German rivalry. For this discussion ice hockey will do. The International Ice Hockey Federation was one of the earliest sport organizations to grant recognition to the DDR, a situation Bonn tried constantly to reverse. In 1961 the West Germans took their team out of the world championships because they feared that East Germany could

beat them, thus necessitating a salute they were unwilling to provide. For this move Bonn was nearly thrown
out of the federation.[34]

Two years later East Germany returned the favor, as
its team turned their backs on their rivals after West
Germany had won a contest between the two. The DDR was
suspended from competition for three months, and was
let back in only after an official statement regretting
this act. It may be that such an apology was forthcoming because the tacit political recognition available
in international sport was too useful to lose. The East
Germans, in any case, claimed that they had not meant to
snub their opponents, merely to salute them in their own
way. They offered to repeat the ceremony.[35]

The German situation eventually became intolerable
to Olympic authorities, who finally decided that arti-
icial amalgamation of two very different Germanies in
one Olympic team had to end. The United States contributed to this perception by insisting, in the early 1960s,
that political sport reflect political reality. Both at
the 1960 Winter Olympics and at the 1962 World Wrestling
Championshis (held in Toledo, Ohio), DDR athletes and
journalists were denied visas on the grounds that they
traveled under a passport not recognized by the United
States.[36] It is interesting that the US would condemn
Canada in 1976 for doing the same thing to Taiwan that
Americans had already done to East Germans fourteen
years earlier. American actions can certainly be explained by the Berlin crisis (the Berlin Wall went up
in August 1961), but the fact remains that this country
was as ready as any to use sport in its diplomatic
interest.

In preparation for Tokyo the two Germanies argued
over the flag. Neither side liked the compromise
banner, but both recognized its political significance
and fought over the issue of who would carry it in the
opening Olympic ceremony. In addition, the West Germans
brought the question of Berlin squarely into its Olympic
context by insisting on holding trials for "unified"
team selection in the divided city.

This was one of a series of moves in which West
Germany reacted to the Wall--which was besides everything else the economic declaration of independence of
the DDR--by asserting its right to jurisdiction over
West Berlin (other steps included holding a meeting
of the Bundestag in the divided capital). The East
Germans chose to boycott the trials rather than to
provide West Germany with a propaganda and publicity
victory. The DDR did send athletes to Tokyo, however, as
Olympic officials authorized some team trials in East
Germany.[37]

East Germany finally was granted full IOC recognition after the 1964 Olympics. East Germans competed in
the "Little Olympics" in Mexico, held in 1965 in order
to test the effects of the high altitude and thin air of
Mexico City on the health and stamina of Olympic athletes, and then marched as a separate team in 1968.

Separate DDR presence in Mexico ended the fiction
of a unified German team, but did not end the rivalry
between the two Germanies in international sport. A
year before those Games Jürgen May, an East German track
star, defected to the Federal Republic. The DDR
charged that he had accepted a bribe from a western
company.[38] The West Germans noted with glee a statement
made by May when he was still a hero across the Wall:
"The path I have taken is typical for the development of
a young man in our state."[39]

Despite such embarrassments, the DDR kept on with
its massive sport program, achieving great success in
intra-German competition before a German audience at the
1972 Olympic Games. The Munich Olympics, held so soon
after East Germany's achieving Olympic recognition, was
a natural outlet for competition between the two states.
Little of the cordiality of "Ostpolitik" (a process by
which West Germany recognized Germany's eastern boundaries and entered a competition with East Germany for
markets and legitimacy in Eastern Europe and the USSR)
applied to relations in Munich, where East Germany
clearly aimed to win more medals than Bonn, and did so
easily. It is hard to say whether or not the 1972 Games
would have been friendlier if the inter-German treaty,
completed later that year, had already been signed.

Marc Hodler, a Swiss member of the International
Ski Federation (East Germany also did well in the 1972
winter Olympics in Sapphoro, Japan) expressed the concern (or admiration) which spread after 1972:

> They (the East Germans) are finding their
> Olympians while they are still in their cradles,
> and they are taking them into full-time camps
> and training them as if they were thorough-bred
> horses or racing dogs.[40]

In 1976 East Germany performed even more spectacu-
larly, winning more gold medals than the United States
and finishing second to the USSR in the standings (this
was the first time the Americans ever finished third).
Flushed with this success, the DDR declared its national
goal to be 50 gold medals in Moscow in 1980. The East
Germans "only" won 47 1980 Olympic events, but that
could hardly be considered a failure. Despite such set-
backs as the 1978 world swimming championships, where the
US women's team upset the East Germans, the DDR continues
to impress the world with its athletes.

72

    To attain these goals, the East Germans have had to
challenge the Soviets in a number of sports. Their
propaganda always mixes domestic celebration with careful recognition of the victories of the other socialist
countries, led by the Soviet Union. The DDR is much
more sensitive to the feelings of Soviet authorities,
athletes, and fans than, say, Yugoslav basketball players or Romanian gymnasts. This is likely to remain the
case.

    In the United States there is a tendancy to admire
East German sport simply on the basis that it produces
champions. The DDR, like other Socialist states, is
proud to advertise its system of mass sport, denying
both that its champions are pampered or that they
artificially augment performance through drugs. In any
case, it should be noted that sport provides one of the
few points of orientation for a regime still extremely
uncertain of its hold on its people and insecure in its
relations with Bonn. The fact that East Germany clearly
won the inter-German sport battle should be considered
in the context of its coming off second best to West
Germany in nearly everything else.

CHINA

    In the contemporary era China has embraced Western
forms of government and political ideology even though
it is a society with a deep cultural and political
heritage independent of Western concepts of political
development. Chinese experiments with capitalism,
militarism, and Marxism-Leninism have led it to
assimilate forms of Western culture as well.
    China was introduced to some forms of Western sport
around the turn of the century, especially through the
efforts of the YMCA.[41] The latter spread Western ideas
on physical culture to segments of the Chinese much as
missionaries spread Christianity. By the 1920's
Western sport influence had reached a point where it
equalled that of Japanese sport in Chinese society.[42]
    Chiang Kai-shek and the Kuomintang took an active
part in the propagation of sport once maximum Nationalist
control was established in the late 1920s. In 1929, the
National Physical Education Law was passed for the
purpose of strengthening human resources in the drive to
develop China's capacity for national defense.[43] The
next year the Government recognized the China Amateur
Athletic Federation as having the primary responsibility
for getting this done. As it turned out, the Japanese
invasion came before national sport could prepare for
national defense; the Nationalists never could complete
their plan to use sport to advance national unity.

By creating a national federation, however, the government enabled China to take part in organized transnational sport. The Chinese joined the Olympic Movement in 1923 (before the Kuomintang had control of northern China), but did not attend a meeting of an Olympic body until 1928. The first Chinese Olympic athlete went to Los Angeles in 1932, but only as a result of the "Manchukuo" controversy noted above.

After this incident Chiang recognized that the Olympics were a political forum, and imported a German coach to train his team. There was a great deal of German influence in China at the time. Hans von Seeckt and other German officers planned some the most success-ful Nationalist attacks against Communist rural bases before World War II. The Chinese delegation to the 1936 Berlin Olympics totaled 107 people; it was the height of Nationalist participation in international sport. In 1948 China sent only seven athletes to London.

The Chinese Communists have also used sport to pro-vide human resources with the strength for national defense, but have had clearer ideological purposes behind their physical culture than the Kuomintang. Contemporary Chinese sport retains significant ties to Mao Zedong even though other aspects of his "Thought" are being discarded. In 1917 Mao wrote "A Study of Physical Education," urging the use of sport for national rejuvination.[44] His pre-Marxist approach to physical culture was the same as that of Father Jahn or the Sokols; the national spirit was to be awakened by means of physical activity.

The Marxist element was added later, and stipulated that Mao's sport had to be mass sport. Physical activ-ity was needed to turn the will to win into the ability to win among people who had to fight enemies who were better armed and more technologically advanced.

The preoccupation with the human element in revolution and war continues to define a difference between Chinese and Soviet sport. The Chinese have the same respect as the Soviets for scientific training methods. They try to learn the most modern methods in each sport from whomever is the best at it. However, while the Soviets greatly stress scientific training and Pavlovian repetition of skills, the Chinese care more about the human will. The Soviets expect their athletes to be well-rounded physically and intellectu-ally, but the Chinese place special emphasis on constant positive ideological reaffirmation on the part of the athlete wishing to demonstrate his or her loyalty.

The political purpose of sport in China is similar to that in Western states. The state seeks loyalty and legitimacy through athletic role models. In the Chinese context, national defense, internal propaganda, and

signals concerning the relative status of the leadership[45] are all enhanced through sport. Where the
Chinese have made an original contribution has been in
their attitude toward athletic diplomacy.

Since the Great Proletarian Cultural Revolution
(GPCR), the slogan "friendship first, competition
second" has been the guiding concept of Chinese sport.
Although this slogan itself is now out of favor China,
unlike the superpowers, recognizes that sporting
opponents can react to defeat with bitterness as well as
awe and admiration.

For the Chinese, the athlete is a different sort of
class ambassador. He or she reaches out to raise the
consciousness of others throughout the world who have
the common framework of the athletic field, but who lack
the common knowledge of Marxism-Leninism. Winning is
not as important as is the process which brings Chinese
athletes together with their opponents. In the world
of political sport, it is class consciousness which
causes victory off the field, and probably on. It is
the duty of the political athlete to spread this Truth
through personal example. Radio Beijing expressed this
policy in 1971, a few months before "Ping Pong Diplomacy."

> Whether or not a team or individual is victorious
> and gains honor depends on whether or not he gives
> prominence to proletarian politics during the
> competition, whether or not he wins in the realm
> of ideology, whether or not he can lose without
> losing the spirit of sportsmanship, and whether
> or not he puts proletarian politics in command
> of the tournament and participates for the sake
> of proletarian politics.[46]

The Chinese expressed nothing but contempt for the
Soviet ("Bourgeois Revisionist") concentration on
winning, a policy which they referred to as "championship mentality." They called it:

> a hideous trick devised by bourgeois revisionism
> to corrupt peoples' souls...a disease which
> poisons the minds of people so that they fight
> for individual fame and profit...a monster which
> tempts people to serve the ruling class.[47]

For all of this, the Chinese did not use the
Olympic system any differently than other states. As
with all countries, China recognized that the Olympic
Games involve questions of prestige and political

recognition. From 1949-1980 the Olympics were a focus of the Chinese drive for the expulsion of the Nationalists, now on Taiwan, from international relations.

Originally, the IOC wanted one China, just as it wanted one Germany. Unlike the German case, however, the IOC could not make up its mind as to which government to recognize. The policies of both Chinas permitted the IOC to shelve this dilemma until after the 1952 Olympics. Taiwan snubbed the Helsinki Games rather than risk being part of a two-China show. Beijing did not belong to five sport federations as required for Olympic participation.[48] The Communists sent a team to the Games anyway, but it arrived too late to compete.

In 1954 the IOC voted 23-21 in favor of admitting the PRC, and it looked as if the PRC would be represented in Melbourne. Peking expressed a desire to participate, but finally boycotted when the IOC refused to drop its insistence on a "two China" policy. Such a policy was as unrealistic in the Olympic Movement as in the rest of international politics. Both "Chinas" were agreed on two things: there was only one China and Taiwan was part of it. The issue turned simply on which government one recognized.

Each superpower campaigned for its own "China." The United States counted on keeping the PRC out of individual federations so that Olympic rules would work against Peking's participation as in 1952. The Soviet Union's representative at the 1954 IOC meeting called the Kuomintang "political leftovers." The Soviet Union continued to press for Chinese entry into the Olympic Games even after the Sino-Soviet split broke into the open.

In 1960 the IOC ended up with no "China" at all. The PRC withdrew its claims from the Olympic Movement in 1958 in protest of the Olympic acceptance of two Chinas.[49] Taiwan pressed for Olympic participation, but ran into problems stemming from the IOC's own political criteria for membership. Since the Nationalists no longer ruled the mainland the IOC refused to let them compete as "China" in Olympic competition.

Taiwan was forced to march its 1960 Olympic team behind a sign reading "Formosa."[50] The Kuomintang considered withdrawal, but needed the political legitimacy of athletic competition. In Rome, one of the athletes marching behind "Formosa" held his own sign reading "Under Protest."

By 1964 the IOC edged back toward recognition of Taiwan as "China." The PRC remained outside the Olympic Movement. It originally concentrated on the idea of a third world sport organization (GANEFO--to

be analyzed in the next chapter), but finally retreated
to itself during the convulsive Great Proletarian Cultural Revolution (GPCR). Lacking two Chinas, the IOC
leaned toward the one which recognized its authority,
and Taiwan's participation was not seriously challenged
again until the 1970's.

The Chinese approach to the third world resumed
once the GPCR ended. But, since the end of GANEFO,
Beijing has waged its battles for proletarian politics
and against Taiwan within the regular channels of
political sport. They have also entered into a more
open relationship with the class enemy, the United
States.

The main impetus behind this was undoubtedly the
Sino-Soviet split. Although the Chinese had established
some sporting contacts with Britain and France, as well
as the third world, their main focus traditionally had
been on relations with other Communist states. However,
the Chinese gradually became as afraid of their
Socialist neighbor as of their class enemy. While the
United States was far away, moreover, the Soviet Union
shared with China the longest common border in the
world, a border which was soon ringed by the largest
concentration of peactime armament in history.

Table tennis was a sport in which Beijing considered
certain American officials to be cooperative. Rufford
Harrison of the US Table Tennis Federation (USTTF) had
voted at an International Table Tennis Federation (ITTF)
meeting in favor of the motion which brought the 1961
world championships to Peking. He had further expressed
the hope that someday his country would allow him to
attend such an event.[51] No member of an offical
American government delegation could have made such a
statement in the early 1960s, or could have voted to
hold a diplomatic event on the Chinese mainland under
Maoist jurisdiction. Harrison told this author that,
at a later ITTF meeting, he was greated with a bear hug
from the leader of the Chinese delegation.[52]

The chances for "Ping Pong Diplomacy" were inter-
rupted by the GPCR, during which Chinese athletes drop-
ped from the international scene. In 1965 Chinese
players won the world table tennis championships.
However, two years later the Chinese team withdrew from
the tournament, and Zuang Zedong, the men's world
champion, disappeared from view.

His reappearance in 1979 (and eventual elevation to
Minister of Sport) signaled the early stages of Chinese
reemergence into world affairs.[53] The next year China
sent its table tennis team to the world championships in
Nagoya, Japan. The Chinese invited the British delegation there to send a team to visit China. It was during
the same competition that Harrison was approached with

a similar offer from Song Chong, leader of the Chinese team.[54] Within a week the Americans were on their way to Beijing. The trip was a highly publicized success which included a series of exhibitions and a meeting with Premier Zhou Enlai. It was followed by more exchanges between the two countries, culminating in President Nixon's 1972 trip to China.

"Ping Pong Diplomacy" was similar in importance to earlier US-Soviet track meets and the USSR gave significant attention to the table tennis exchange in its press.[55] It was a warning signal to the Soviets regarding a new factor in its triangular relationship with the PRC and US.

As with Soviet-American meets, repeating the process merely made the event more commonplace and, therefore, less politically dramatic. Still, subsequent exchanges of gymnasts, basketballers, and other athletes prepared the US and Chinese publics to accept the idea of normal relations with what had been an arch enemy.

By themselves, of course, such sport exchanges could not alter diplomatic relations. Sport, being politically peripheral, was of no use when it came to differences in attitude toward such issues as Taiwan and US-Soviet detente. China, disappointed until recently with American policy on both scores, showed that sport could open up relationships with other countries as well.

China arranged track meets with Italy, Rumania, and Spain in 1975. As early as 1971, "Ping Pong Diplomacy" was extended to Yugoslavia. Two Communist states with a history of independence from Soviet policy demonstrated that Moscow would not be able to count on an end to their deviations. Albania, as well as the USSR, was concerned with improved Sino-Yugoslav ties. The latter were early signals of cooler Sino-Albanian relations.

This Chinese sport offensive of the 1970's had one unexpected facet. In June 1973 it was announced that a table tennis team from Taiwan would be invited to Beijing.[56] No answer from the Nationalists was recorded. Despite this ploy, directed at a Taiwan which could be counted on to turn it down, the main Chinese drive against Taiwan actually heated up. Renewed Chinese interest in the international sport system was accompanied by demands for Taipei's ouster. China increased the number of federations to which it belonged at the same time that it increased its diplomatic representation in the West, and always insisted that each federation expel Taiwan from its ranks. By 1974 China had joined, among others, the fencing, swimming, volleyball, and ice hockey groups. The latter sport was the medium by which Peking made an abortive approach to Canada, the next Olympic host.[57] In April 1975 Beijing applied for membership in the International Lawn Tennis Federation and expressed interest in Davis Cup competition (Jiang Qing of "Gang of Four" fame considered tennis particularly bourgeois and this may have been a slap at her).[58] In September, the Chinese were admitted to the World University Games Federation.[59]

The Chinese had more trouble in other sports. After Taiwan was ousted from, and Peking admitted to, the Asian Games Federation, China became eligible for the 1974 Asian Games in Tehran. However, the International Association Football (soccer) Federation refused to oust Taipei. In return, Peking refused to allow the federation a "two China" policy.[60] China was barred from track and field for the same reason. So China could go to Tehran, but could only compete in those sports in which it had federation membership.

The Chinese decided that their presence in Tehran was important enough to try to appear in as many sports as possible, and did make accommodations with some groups. The swimming body, for example, allowed Chinese athletes to compete while China allowed the federation to table the Taiwan question.[61]

China sent a 270 member delegation to Iran and won more medals than any country besides Japan. Chinese athletes demonstrated, however, that "Friendship First, Competition Second" was a doctrine dependent of the political situation. The PRC refused to play tennis or fence against Israel.[62] Chinese medal winners refused to shake the hands of any Israelis sharing medal winner pedestals with them. China claimed that this was done in order not to offend Iraq. In fact, China merely extended its political policy into a forum where it could be publicly demonstrated. The natural connection between sport and politics was used by a government in the process of reentering the international system in both activities.

The Olympic Games, being a primary form of political sport, was the next target of Chinese sport diplomacy. In April 1975 it was reported that the IOC would look favorably on a Chinese application.[63] China took the hint and, being a member of more than the five federations required for Olympic participation, applied for admission to the Olympics.[64] In preparing for the Moscow Olympics, however, the issue of Taiwan remained a problem. China seemed content to oust Taipei in federation after federation, while it waited for the IOC to end its "two China" policy.

This process was probably accelerated by the fact that the next two Olympic hosts were states having no diplomatic relations with Taiwan. Canada extended this diplomatic fact to its sport policy when it refused to

allow Taipei's 1976 Olympic team to enter the country
under passports reading "Republic of China."[65] In
addition, Canada barred Taiwan from flying its flag in
the Olympic display. American threats to boycott the
Games and IOC motions to transfer them were irrelevent;
Canada merely made an appropriate (in terms of previous
Olympic policy and diplomatic conduct) demonstration of
its foreign policy. The IOC eventually backed off and
offered Nationalist athletes the chance to march behind
the Olympic banner. Taiwan refused to accept this, as
it would have involved diminution of its legitimacy and
violation of its foreign policy.

In July 1976 the tenth anniversary of one of Mao's
famous swims was celebrated throughout China.[66] Bathers
were reported to have called for the Chairman to live
10,000 years.[67] Mao himself was too feeble to swim, a
fact which may have alerted the public to the extent of
his physical disability. His passing brought all
Chinese policies, including "Friendship First, Competition Second" into question. How future Chinese sport
attitudes and slogans will unfold will depend on the
perceived relationships between the new leaders'
policies and the use of sport in public diplomacy. In
the meantime there was the 1980 Moscow Olympics, which
will be treated separately.

NOTES

1. Olympic Newsletter, #16 (January, 1969),
p. 39.
2. Weyand, The Olympic Pagent, p. 283.
3. New York Times, December 5, 1948, December,
6, 1948.
4. See David B. Kanin, "Superpower Sport in Cold
War and Detente," in B. Lowe, D.B. Kanin, and A. Strenk,
ed., Sport and International Relations (Champaign, Ill.,
Stipes, 1978), pp. 249-262.
5. The Times (London), August 22, 1946).
6. Ivor Montagu, East-West Sport Relations
(Peace Pamphlet #52) (London: National Peace Council,
1951), pp. 16-17.
7. The Times (London), April 8, 1948.
8. The Times (London), September 9, 1948.
9. New York Times, May 15, 1950.
10. J.N. Washburn, "Sport as a Soviet Tool,"
Foreign Affairs XXXIV, #3 (April, 1956) p. 498.
11. The Times, (London), December 29, 1952.
12. Philip Goodhart and Christopher Chataway,
War Without Weapons (London: W.H. Allen, 1968), p. 46.
13. New York Times, January 27, 1952.
14. New York Times, February 20, 1952.
15. The Times (London), July 21, 1952.

16. New York Times, July 22, 1952.

17. New York Times, April 20, 1952.

18. Johnson, All That Glitters is not Gold, p. 221.

19. Current Digest of the Soviet Press (CDSP) IV, #31, Pravda, July 31, 1952.

20. Nikolai Tarasov, Soviet Sport Today (Moscow: Novosti, 1964), p. 45.

21. Author interview with Daniel Ferris, Executive-Secretary Emeritus of the AAU, November 30, 1973.

22. Sports Illustrated, XI, #5 (August 3, 1959), p. 31.

23. Sports Illustrated, XII, #10 (March 7. 1960), p. 14

24. New York Times, May 23, 1959

25. New York Times, June 5, 1962.

26. Sports Illustrated, XXV, #3 (July 18, 1966), p. 12.

27. Sports Illustrated, XXVIII, #15 (April 15, 1968), p. 29

28. The Times (London), October 23, 1968.

29. The Times (London), May 23, 1951.

30. The Times, (London), November 16, 1951.

31. New York Times, May 10, 1951, May 11, 1951.

32. New York Times, February 9, 1952.

33. New York Times, June 26, 1955.

34. The Times (London), March 15, 1961.

35. The Times (London), March 18, 1963.

36. Sports Illustrated, XVII, #3 (June 18, 1962), p. 10.

37. New York Times, August 2, 1963.

38. Sports Illustrated, XXVII, #6 (August 7, 1967), p. 12.

39. Ibid.

40. Johnson, All That Glitters is not Gold, p. 38.

41. Jonathon Kolatch, Sport, Politics, and Ideology in China (Middle Village, N.Y.: Jonathon David, 1972), pp. 7-9.

42. Ibid., pp. 32-3.

43. Ibid.

44. Mao Tse-tung, "A Study of Physical Education," in S. Schramm, ed., The Political Thought of Mao Tse-tung (NY: Praeger, 1969), pp. 152-160.

45. David B. Kanin, "Ideology and Diplomacy: The International Dimension of Chinese Sport," in Lowe, Kanin, and Strenk, Sport and International Relations. p. 266.

46. Radio Peking, July 27, 1971, quoted in China Notes, #421 (August 16, 1961).

47. Ibid.

48. Kolatch, Sport, Politics, and Ideology in China, p. 170.

49. See Olympic Review, #66-67 (May-June, 1973), pp. 171-174.

50. Ibid.

51. Author interview with Rufford Harrison, December, 13, 1973.

52. Ibid.

53. Sports Illustrated, XXXII, #7 (February 16, 1970), p. 7.

54. Rufford Harrison in Chemical Technology, May, 1972, pp. 276-279.

55. CDSP, XXIII, #16, pp. 20-21, Literaturnaya Gazeta, April 21, 1971.

56. New York Times, June 30, 1973.

57. New York Times, November 27, 1973.

58. New York Times, April 11, 1975.

59. New York Times, November 17, 1975.

60. New York Times, November 20, 1975.

61. New York Times, September 22, 1973.

62. Sports Illustrated, XLI, #12 (September 23, 1974), pp. 61-63.

63. New York Times, April 14, 1975.

64. New York Times, April 18, 1975.

65. New York Times, July 2, 1976.

66. New York Times, July 17, 1976.

67. Ibid.

6

The Emerging Forces

The rest of the world has awakened to the uses of political power in the Western sense, and of sport as a means of demonstrating that power. New states can use sport as easily as old; on the playing field a representative of a weak state usually can defeat one from a stronger political power without fear of political reprisal.

Indeed, for a new state sport can be even more important than for an older one. Many of the "third world" countries have achieved independence on the basis of boundaries corresponding more to lines of colonial administration than to ethnic reality. It can be difficult to create identification with the state in the minds of people with a more narrow orientation. States composed of different nations and lacking the kind of legitimacy usually gained through centuries of authority and strife need tools with which to build a "patriotic" consciousness.

Sport can be one of these tools. Citizens can be trained to be fans, and successful athletes can be used for the benefit of new regimes in search of popularity. Since sport has no intrinsic political value the new leaders can advertise any ideology or "cult of personality" they choose. What the Greek royal family found attractive in the Olympic myth in 1896 many newly emerging states find useful in international sport today.

ASIA

Japan was the first non-Western country to use sport as a tool in Westernization of its society. Strictly speaking Japan was not a newly emerging force. Its islands were populated by people of relatively high cultural homogeneity with a political heritage older than most Olympic founders. Its ancient traditions included forms of ritualized martial art that played a formal role in the life of the society. With the turn to the West during and after the Meiji restoration came the adoption of Western forms of sport. Japan, far from seeking an alternative to Western athletics (as some states would do)

Even so, it took a fairly long time for Western-style sport organization to take root. Japan had put up swimmers to compete against the English in 1848,[1] but the main thrust of sport development did not begin until 1867. The Japanese Amateur Athletic Association was founded only in 1925 and, although the Japanese had taken part in international meets before World War I, it was not until 1932 that Japan became a first-class Olympic power. In this period golf and baseball became great favorites in Japan, and the early trips of American baseball teams to that country were among the earliest examples of the use of sport as a tool in public diplomacy.

Even then, Western sport had to share the stage with traditional activities. Japanese sumo wrestling and martial arts were not phased out, but were encouraged to flourish in the midst of the introduction of new sports.

The fact that cultural pollinization did not prevent the US and Japan from going to war demonstrated the limits of this sort of cultural diplomacy, limits which equally apply to the rhetoric so lavishly laid down in the wake of American sport contacts with the Soviets, Chinese, and Cubans. Japan's attempts to secure the recognition of "Manchukuo" at the 1932 Olympics and the 1934 Far Eastern Games were natural uses of Western political sport. When these initiatives were rejected, it was also natural for Japan to feel discriminated against by the other great powers, and drop its chance to host the 1940 Olympics in favor of more pressing concerns in Asia.

After World War II, however, sport was an important tool in the guided restoration of Japan. Olympic veteran MacArthur ordered baseball competition renewed, and arranged for participation of Japanese swimmers in American meets.[2] He used sport in a conscious effort to make sure that American values took hold at all levels of Japanese society.

The result was the explosion of American sport in Japan. To some extent, there was the creation of a paternalistic attitude in the US concerning Japanese sport and society. The American public was treated to reports which made fun of the Japanese use of English sport terms; at one point Sports Illustrated ridiculed alleged expressions of disbelief by Japanese responding to the victory of the Brooklyn Dodgers in the 1955 World Series.[3]

The American influence on Japanese sport has been overwhelming. Although coaches from many Western states have been imported to teach sport to the Japanese, the American dominance of Japanese society has left an indelible imprint. Reportedly, Japan is one of the few places besides the US where a child will try to catch (rather than kick) a ball when it is thrown to him or her.[4]

When Japan finally did become the first non-Western Olympic host (Australia is certainly closer in culture to Europe than Asia), it did not mean that any great change in Olympic tradition was in the offing. The 1964 Olympic Games were a typically Western event, barely touched by elements of Japan's own cultural heritage. Japan left a legacy of efficiency rather than cultural enrichment, which suited the Olympic Movement just fine.

A more independent position on sport did soon appear, however, just as the Tokyo Games were under preparation. The focus of an alternative model to the Olympic system was taking place in Indonesia. President Sukarno used sport to create an atmosphere for his leadership of non-aligned and "newly-emerging" states. He tried to galvanize his people in opposition to the existence of neighboring Malaysia and to the domination of Southeast Asia by those countries which had colonized much of it in previous centuries. Sukarno was also interested in distracting his people from serious internal economic and social difficulties.

Under the Dutch, Indonesia had little in the way of an organized heritage in Western ideas of physical culture or sport. It was actually the Japanese who created the basis of an Indonesian sport program during their World War II occupation of the then "Dutch East Indies."[5] Sukarno was quick to see the political uses of sport and established an Indonesian Olympic Committee soon after independence. His country was well-represented at the first Asian Games in 1951 (successor the Far Eastern Games organization that had died after the Japan-China squabble over Manchukuo in 1934), and at each Olympic Games starting the following year.

As Sukarno moved more into his policy of "guided democracy," sport became one of the instruments used to bring as much political activity as possible under central control. With the award of the Fourth Asian Games to Djakarta (1962), a Sport Movement Task Force was created to organize them and plan for Indonesian team development.[6]

At these Games, Sukarno tried to establish his image as a leader of the "third world." Indonesia barred Israel and Taiwan from competition in his Asian

Games on the basis of political support for the Arabs
and the People's Republic of China. As a result,
Indonesia was threatened with expulsion from the next
Olympic Games.

Sukarno, rather than being cowed, took the offensive. He called for a new sport organization which
would represent the emerging states of the world. An
Indonesian spokesman expressed his government's view of
the role of sport in politics:

> Pak Bandrio (Indonesian Foreign Minister) has
> clearly said that sports cannot be separated from
> politics. Therefore let us work for a sports
> organization on the basis of politics.[7]

Indonesia, like other non-Western states, did not
come into the world encumbered with all the cultural
baggage of founding Olympic members. Greek tradition
meant nothing to states that did not claim to have
gained anything at Marathon; indeed some of those people
probably had ancestors who fought on the other side.
Sukarno's break with Western sport movements was
interesting in that he tried to create an organization
based on vastly different political assumptions.

What came out of this was the Games of the Newly
Emerging Forces (GANEFO). This was not meant to be a
single athletic meet, but rather a permanent organization
which would celebrate the physical prowess of people
from the third world. Sukarno attacked the IOC as being
an imperialistic organ of a quarter of the world's
population in their attempt to retain control of the
other three-quarters.[8]

Sukarno soon brought his own goals into the sporting struggle. He stepped up pressure on Malaysia through
his GANEFO organ, picturing the new state as an outpost
of imperialism in Southeast Asia.

With Western imperialism the stated enemy, Sukarno
went to the rival Communist giants for aid. The USSR
agreed to foot the bill for the erection of a 100,000
seat stadium, a 10,000 seat "sport palace," and an
8,000 swimming pool complex.[9] The Soviet Union was
cautious in its approach, however, and did not join
GANEFO until six months after its creation.[10] It did
want to enhance its image in the newly emerging states,
but did not want to go so far as to be thrown out of
the Olympic Movement. The latter was too natural a
forum for political prestige to be lost. Nevertheless,
all Communist states were represented in the new
organization by the time it held its first meet in 1963.

The Chinese did not have the same reticence as the
Soviets in their policy toward GANEFO. They enthusiastically built up the latter as being more politically

acceptable than the Olympic Movement which, after all, they had quit some five years before.[11] GANEFO was started partly as a result of Sukarno's pro-Beijing leanings, and the Chinese were effusive in their appreciation for the Indonesian stance on Taiwan.

Sukarno did all he could to flatter and encourage Beijing when GANEFO held its opening ceremony in October 1963. He singled out the PRC delegation for a special greeting, and invited Chinese Vice-Premier Ho Lung to sit with him on the reviewing stand as the teams marched by, an honor shared by no other delegation.[12]

These Games themselves were a strangely mixed affair. Sukarno, as the guiding spirit, used them for the expression of the many nuances of his foreign policy. As a result, while the Games were supposed to be for the progressive states, Sukarno permitted Indonesia's former colonial masters, the Dutch, a place in Djakarta.

The Chinese delegation remained the most vocal during GANEFO and also won the most medals. The Soviets, meanwhile, watched as Beijing turned their investment against them. GANEFO lasted twelve days and ended in a demonstration that, when it came to sport, the newly emerging forces and their fans shared certain behavioral patterns with the imperialists: The United Arab Republic-North Korea soccer match resulted in a riot.

After the Games were over Chinese exuberance continued unabated. It went so far that some concluded that China, not Indonesia, was the leading GANEFO booster.[13]

China Sport devoted an entire issue to GANEFO, and ran photographs of Zhou Enlai and Liu Shaoqi congratulating Sukarno. Indonesian and Chinese messages in support of GANEFO were quoted at length.[14] There was, of course, no mention of any Soviet support for the movement. For both the Chinese and the Indonesians GANEFO proved to be an event which cost little and resulted in great international prestige. Only the USSR, which poured money into the GANEFO host only to have itself shunted aside in favor of its Communist rival, could have any cause for regret.

GANEFO did create some problems for Japan, the next Olympic host. The IOC and the Asian Games federation had sparked GANEFO in the first place by attempting to punish Indonesia for keeping Asian Games member states out of Djakarta in 1962. Sukarno showed himself to be contemptuous of the Olympics. IOC threats against him had no more effect than those of United Nations officials (who he snubbed by deciding to leave that organization as well).

When the IOC announced its intention to oust all
GANEFO contestants from the 1964 Olympics, Japan faced
the possibility of an Afro-Asian boycott of its
expensive investment. As it turned out, the IOC backed
off enough from its position to allow most GANEFO states
to send their athletes to Tokyo. Only the North Koreans
refused to keep athletes who had been in Djakarta away
from the 1964 Olympics, and thus boycotted the latter
(sending to Tokyo only an avalanche of propaganda).
China stayed on the sidelines and supported the Olympic
boycott threat.

As originally conceived, GANEFO was going to be an
ongoing movement, and plans for GANEFO II soon were made
public. The second meeting of the GANEFO governing
board was held in Bejing in September 1965, with thirty-
nine states in attendance. The delegates chose Cairo as
the site for GANEFO II, with Beijing as the alternative
host. China Sport singled out the PRC, the Arab states,
Indonesia, Mongolia, North Vietnam, and North Korea as
the "leaders" of the movement. The Soviets, in contrast
to the "leaders," were credited simply with having
attended.15

GANEFO II never came to pass. Sukarno was over-
thrown after the bloody failure of the Indonesian
Communist Party coup in 1965. His successors suspended
the struggle against Malaysia, wiped out the Indonesian
Communists, and moved the country back toward the
mainstream of international politics and away from
GANEFO. The Indonesian Olympic committee was recreated
in 1967,and Djakarta rejoined the Olympic movement (and
the United Nations) in time for the Mexico City Olympic
Games in 1968.

Cairo had to withdraw its bid to host GANEFO II;
the Egyptians could not handle the financial strain
and Nasser was preparing for a more direct form of
political opposition to Israel, resulting in the disaster
of the Six-Day War. Beijing, the alternative site, also
had to relinquish its right to GANEFO due to the fact
that the Great Proletarian Cultural Revolution caused
too much chaos and dislocation for China to allow a
public international sport spectacle to take place within
its borders.

GANEFO was thus shorn of its major political backers
before it could institutionalize its celebrations.
Other meets were held under its auspices, but they could
not recreate the feeling of 1963. GANEFO's legacy was
one of challenge to the Olympic Movement through the
recognition of the connection of sport and politics.
It represented an interesting attempt to create an
international organization challenging the organs of
developed states in a public arena.

The model that Sukarno himself provided was
followed by another flamboyant Asian leader, Cambodia's
Prince Norodom Sihanouk. Sihanouk flirted with GANEFO
at the same time that neighboring Thailand was awarded
the fifth Asian Games in 1966.[16] He hosted one of the
last GANEFO meetings in December 1966.

Unlike Sukarno, Sihanouk was prone to personal
athletic posturing. He claimed to be the leading basketball and volleyball player in his country' in one basketball game it was claimed that he scored 92 points. His
fall from power seemed the end of a brilliant athletic
career. It certainly was the end of GANEFO.

Third world Olympic Committees gravitated back
toward the Olympic Movement, but made an attempt to
reform its structure. After the 1968 Olympics Communist
and third world Committees tried to organize a Permanent
General Assembly (PGA) of NOCs. The PGA, created in
Mexico City during the Olympic year, was billed to
developed states' Olympic officials at the NOC's
version of the General Assembly of International
Federations (GAIF). The GAIF increasingly wrested
authority and responsbility from the IOC, and some NOC
heads hoped the PGA could do the same. However, it soon
became clear that third world and Soviet officials wanted
to use the PGA to become dominant throughout the Olympic
Movement. PGA advocates pressed this aspect of their
case too strongly at the 1969 Dubrovnik IOC Executive
Board meeting, turning many officials against the
concept. As a result, the PGA was discredited. NOCs
still lack a unified structure on GAIF lines.[17]

CUBA

The politics of Latin American sport have been
different than Asian sport because of the political,
economic, and geographic presence of the United States.
The North Americans have dominated much of hemispheric
sport in the same way that the US has been the dominant
political power in the region. Some sports, however,
have provided a means for the Latin Americans to
demonstrate that the North Americans can be beaten.

The most popular sport in the region, and the world,
is association football. It is the epitome of Latin
American sport and is an activity passionately followed
in Latin America on a national basis. As early as 1936
the newly elected President of Brazil, Oscar Benavides,
urged his national team to increase public identification with the team and to "maintain to the utmost the
prestige of the national colors."[18]

The popularity of this sport caused two observers (Edgell and Jary) to attempt to determine whether it would supercede other sports in a country once it took root.[19] An Argentinian Marxist, Juan Jose Sebrelli, worried about soccer superceding other activities as well. He complained that soccer taught people to be passive.[20] To him, the game kept Latin American masses in a state of primative emotionalism. Sebrelli specifically alleged that the victory of a Buenos Aires soccer team took the masses' attention away from the death of Che Guevara. In short, soccer, rather than religion, was fast becoming the opium of the people.

Other Marxists, however, have found that sport can be useful in orienting mass perceptions of national power and political will. Since 1959 Cuba, ruled by a baseball pitcher named Fidel Castro, has used sporting activity to impress the workers with Cuban prowess and to demonstrate excellence in a hostile regional climate.

Cuba has provided a serious challenge to United States hegemony in the hemisphere. Castro's government has been the object of constant political harrassment and economic blockade since he became an avowed commuist. For his part, Fidel has sought to export his revolution, first throughout the rest of the hemisphere, and lately in Africa as well.

On the other hand, sport is one of the few forms of international relations through which there have been regular contacts between Cuba and the United States. It has been a forum for propaganda as well as athletics; representative athletes have engaged in ideological and other forms of competition.

Cuba competed in the Ninth Central American and Caribbean Games in 1962, even though it was in the process of being ousted from the Organization of American States (OAS). In using this event as a political forum, Castro was reported to have also tried to prepare his athletes against the dangers the Capitalists would tempt them with--women, marijuana, and drugged coffee.[21]

Despite further political and economic sanctions, the peripheral status of sport made it possible for the Capitalists to allow Cuban participation in the Pan-American Games. The public nature of sport turned these Games into an intense struggle for victory and prestige between Cuba and the United States. For the former, these activities could be even more important than the Olympics. In the Pan-American Games Cuba did not have to compete against many of the world's greatest athletic states, and even the United States did not always send its best team. Cuba could train hard for these Games, perform well in "head-to-head" competition with the US, and make a great impression on the rest of the hemisphere. Castro could use sport to demonstrate that his

small country was not intimidated by the North American
giant, and that his small population could more than
hold its own in the competition for athletic victory.

In 1963 the US lost the Pan-American Games basketball title to Cuba. Sports Illustrated offered one
explanation for the defeat, the traditional one blaming
everything on the fractionalized American team
selection process.[22] That magazine expressed a sense
of national embarrassment based on the assumption that
the country which invented a sport should continue to
dominate it. Cuban-American rivalry continued to dominate succeeding Pan-American competitions, leading to
impressive Cuban showings in track and field, baseball,
and other sports besides basketball.

In recent Olympiads Cuba has improved its global
sporting performance as well. Alberto Juantorena was
perhaps the outstanding track performer at the 1976
Montreal Olympics and, along with such athletes as
Silvio Leonard, has made Cuba a first-rate track power.
In boxing, a sport perhaps closest to mimicing the kind
of political rivalry represented by international sport,
the 1976 Cuban team finished second only to the United
States. The 1980 team did even better, clearly benefit-
ting from the US boycott.

Despite the animosity, sport still managed to serve
as a means of contact between the US and Cuba. Castro
himself has stayed interested in American baseball while
periodically taking part in Havana contests (he was the
subject of the following American baseball scouting
report: "Fair fast ball, good control, no curve ball.
Strictly Class D material").[23] It was reported that
Castro sent players to Canada to watch North American
teams on television.[24]

The sporting "thaw" between the US and Cuba has been
more hesitant than that between the United States and
its larger communist adversaries. In 1973, at the World
University Games in Moscow, the Cubans, about to lose a
basketball contest with the US, picked up some chairs
and started a fight with their opponents. However, in
1974 Cuba allowed the American Broadcasting Company to
televise the World Weightlifting Championships from
Havana. American and Cubans also cooperated in the
filming of the World Amateur Boxing Championships, held
in Havana in September of that year.

In December 1974 it was reported that Canada and
Cuba had come to a major sport agreement. Canada
wanted to train athletes in a warm climate, one which
allowed the outdoor regimen many of them needed. Cuba
agreed to provide such a climate for 139 Canadian
athletes who took part in many matches against their
Cuban hosts.[25]

At the same time, the Cuban national basketball team was competing in Franco's Spain against the highly-rated team from the University of North Carolina. Castro was dropping hints that he wanted more normal relations with the US, and increased use of sport underlined his intentions. In April 1975 the Cuban representative at the International Amateur Baseball Federation was quoted as saying that his country intended to invite US major league teams to tour the island (such competition between amateurs and professionals would require the sanction of the federation).[26]

The next month Senator George McGovern came out in favor of a trip of American baseball and basketball players to Cuba.[27] McGovern also helped in the arrangements which sent the parents of Cuban-born American pitcher Luis Tiant to the US for the 1975 season (and subsequent world series).

Since 1975 exchanges with the Cubans have taken place in a number of sports. The competition at the 1976 Olympics spurred interest in particular in boxing, and Cuban-American matches have been held a number of times. When in Cuba these fights are attended by Castro himself, who once allowed himself to be interviewed by a particularly ingratiating Howard Cosell. In addition, McGovern arranged for two collegiate basketball teams from South Dakota to visit Cuba, a trip which disappointed the hosts because the caliber of the visitors was clearly not conducive to exciting basketball.

Even though sport exchanges between the US and Cuba have received a fair amount of publicity, they have not served as politically ground-breaking events in the sense of earlier exchanges between the United States, USSR, and China. This is because in the Cuban case ground was already broken by other than sporting means, and because the US and Cuba had a severe falling out soon after the first sporting contacts took place. In the Soviet and Chinese cases, on the other hand, sport served as one of th few means by which the US and its communist adversaries carried on a public relationship.

Cuba, like China, had no diplomatic relations with the United States when sporting exchanges commenced. But in the Cuban case, sport soon was overshadowed by other forms of political approach. Senators Pell, Javits, and McGovern went to Cuba in 1975. Their trips were well-publicized and opened the idea of more normal diplomatic ties with Cuba to public scrutiny. In addition, in 1975 Secretary of State Kissinger spoke out on the subject of ending the US embargo against Cuba.[28] There were also significant improvements in relations between Cuba and the OAS.

As a sport exchanges continue, their political
importance decreases in terms of each exchange itself.
People soon get used to these events and pay less
attention to them. Therefore, when Cuban-American
relations cooled dramatically following Cuba's contribution to civil wars and revolutions in Africa, sport
could provide little in the way of dramatic "good will"
to defuse the tension.

This situation was somewhat similar to the virtually
unnoticed resumption of US-Soviet track and field meets
after 1969. Sport exchanges may in the future demonstrate better hemispheric relations, but will be able to
do so only as progress becomes evident in the main forum
of political struggle. In the meantime, Cuba will
continue to perform impressively at the Olympic Games
and in regional sport, and will likely use athletic
achievement to stress its ties with the Soviet bloc.
In 1984, as in 1976 and 1980, the Cubans will probably
catagorize their achievements as part of the collective
medal-winning process of socialist sport.

MEXICO, THE SUPERPOWERS, AND THE 1968 OLYMPIC GAMES

Mexico was the first third world state to host an
Olympic Games. It received the 1968 award despite
charges that the thin air at Mexico City's high altitude
made it dangerous for athletes to compete. The IOC
dismissed this concern, and clearly recognized the
political importance of the award. Avery Brundage went
out of his way to claim that the Olympic Movement was
making a contribution to what he termed "the most stable
and fastest growing country in Latin America."[29]

The 1968 Olympics were a demonstration that a newly
emerging state with small international teams could use
sport for the same purposes as established sport powers.
Mexico had an advantage over many other third world
states in that it had a national tradition of nearly a
century and a half to rely on in its Olympic preparation.

What the Mexican government had in mind, therefore,
was not so much the cementing of popular identification
with the state as government capitalization on Mexico's
perception of a revolutionary heritage. While Cuba had
its active struggle with the United States to fuel
political identity, Mexico had to fall back on a heritage
increasingly too far in the past to be remembered by its
citizens. Mexico could claim to have been the site of
the first of the great revolutions of the twentieth
century, and used the Olympic Games to remind its own
people of its progressive tradition.

This conscious attempt to promote Mexico's revolutionary image incurred the wrath of some Mexicans who
felt that the government had betrayed the country's

revolutionary roots. Certain Mexican students considered their country to be a lackey of the United States and a practitioner of domestic repression. They were particularly angry at the government for holding hundreds of what they believed to be political prisoners. The students as well as the government recognized the political content of Olympic preparation, and ten days before the opening of the Games the two sides squared off in a series of confrontations.

Demonstrations for the release of political prisoners soon turned into a bloody riot (whether started by students or police is not clear). At least 200 students were reported killed when police finally invaded student ranks to stop the embarrassing events.[30]

The students used the Games to show that the regime was neither as stable nor as progressive as advertised. The huge numbers of reporters in Mexico for the Olympics provided the perfect opportunity for the dissidents to display their grievances before an international audience. For the government, on the other hand, once the riots were put down the Games could be used for purposes originally conceived. While television showed murals by Trotsky's friend Diego Rivera, the Mexican organizers showed the world that they could run an impressive athletic show. In future Games, third world hosts and their political opponents will have ample opportunity to give a mass audience a lesson in whatever fuels the grievances between them.

1968 was also an interesting Olympic year in that it provided examples of sporting conflict between established Olympic powers and their own athletic dissidents. The United States was in the midst of turmoil revolving around the Vietnam War and Civil War Rights movement. While the former was heating up, the latter was perceived to be grinding to a halt. Some black Americans felt frustrated that the great hopes of the early part of the decade seemed to be dying away, both as a result of rising preoccupation with Vietnam and a so-called white backlash against civil rights reforms. The murder of Martin Luther King seemed to galvanize this frustration, resulting not only in urban riots but also in campaigns to move black people away from reliance on the "American system."

One of the most noted means for black social mobility was achievement in sport. Since Jesse Owens, blacks used athletic victory as a lever for individual recognition and social prestige. In 1968, however, some American black athletes and scholars tried to convince their fellows that the best way to use political sport was as a protest against the government, not a celebration of it. Dr. Harry Edwards, a sociologist, led a movement designed to lead American black athletes into a

more protective use of their talents. He wanted them
to boycott the 1968 Olympic Games as a demonstration of
their displeasure with US policy. Edwards recognized
the political meaning of national uniforms, teams,
flags, and anthems, and sought to use a boycott of them
to protest what he felt was a betrayal of black people
by their rulers.

The boycott movement fizzled, due probably to
Edwards' loss of rapport with some athletes and to the
lure of international competition and Olympic prestige.
Still, some blacks stayed out of the Games, and in
Mexico John Carlos and Tommie Smith staged a silent
protest after winning medals in the 100 meter dash.
During the playing of the United States national
anthem, they bowed their heads and raised gloved fists.
For this action they were booed by the crowd and thrown
out of the Games by the IOC and US Olympic Committee.

The IOC, of course, viewed this protest as a
violation of Olympic tenets as well as good taste.
In fact, however, this non-violent demonstration was as
legitimate a use of political sport as any by Olympic
states. Smith and Carlos used the Games to advocate
political change in the same fashion as the rest of the
Olympic athletes use them to celebrate the political
status quo.

As with other forms of political sport, repetition
of this type of protest resulted in far less political
impact. In 1972 Wayne Collett and Vince Matthews managed
to get themselves thrown out of the Munich Olympics for
an act similar to Carlos and Smith's. Hardly anybody
noticed.

On the night of August 20-21, 1968 Warsaw Pact
armies invaded Czechoslovaia. This act followed months
of political wrangling between the latter and other
socialist states based on what came to be known as the
"Prague Spring." Among those leading the reform move
in Czechoslovakia was Emil Zatopek, star of the 1948
and 1952 Olympic Games. Zatopek helped publicize regime
reforms, and at one point even signed a petition urging
the Dubcek government to accelerate their implementation.[31] After the invasion, Zatopek went on television
to urge that the Soviet Union and its fellow invaders
be barred from Olympic competition. For this he was
demoted from his comfortable position in Czechoslovak
sport, but only through a gradual process designed to
minimize popular demonstrations in his behalf.

The USSR did not have to suffer through any
incidents in Mexico resembling the Smith-Carlos affair,
but Soviet and Warsaw Pact athletes were kept separate
from their Czechoslovak colleagues in the Olympic
village in order to minimize the chances for any incidents. Major Soviet embarrassment came later, at the

1969 World Ice Hockey Championships, where they were
beaten by the Czechoslavaks, resulting in a new round
of riots in Prague and in the final demotion of
Alexander Dubcek.

Sport is one of the few international processes in
which East Europeans can challenge Soviet representatives
for the public amusement of their national fans. Subsequent actions of Romanian gymnasts and Yugoslav basketball players as well as Hungarian water polo players
provide a pattern of political challenge to Soviet
domination through one of the only outlets safe to use.

SOUTH AFRICA: SPORT AS A DIPLOMATIC WEAPON

Africa, particularly sub-Saharan Africa, is composed
of states created with artifical boundaries (in ethnic
terms) stemming from divisions of colonial administration. These frontiers are the last, most stubborn
vestiges of Africa's imperial past. Governments succeeding to power in Africa cling to their borders with
as much fervor as their power, since both represent the
image of "modernization," the concept that non-Western
cultures should develop political, social, and economic
institutions mimicing European and North American
history. It is no accident, therefore, that members of
the Organization of African Unity (OAU) immediately find
fault with anyone wanting to change those frontiers,
since that could lead to a flood of ethnic activity
engulfing what is still a tenuous political system.

In such circumstances it is not surprising that
sport is used to solidify citizen identification with the
state. Centralized sport establishments give lip-service
to Olympic mythology in international competition while
using domestic sport to create rigid ideological and
political lines having nothing to do with Western
concepts of "Olympism."

Upon achieving independence, African states found
that they could compete more successfully in the Olympic
Games than in the struggle for resources and power.
International successes spurred the development of
athletic programs and the near-deification of sport
heroes. Abebe Bikela was promoted from private to
lieutenant in the Ethiopian army after he won the second
of his two consecutive Olympic marathons in 1964.[32]
His superior, a colonel, was given the task of arranging
Bikela's schedule so that he could be used as a national
asset and could aid in Ethiopia's sport program. In
other words, the lieutenant had a colonel for a secretary.

Perhaps the most successful use of sport in Africa
for purposes of national orientation has come in Kenya.
For the past twenty years this country has provided

the world with some of its greatest middle distance
runners. The most famous of these was Kipchoge Keino.
His victories in the international glare of the Olympic
Games made him a national hero. It was reported that in
Kenya his presence at a function was usually greeted
with cries of "Harambee" (let's all pull together).[33]
He helped his countrymen say with pride, "I am a Kenyan,"
a notable victory for a government seeking to displace
more traditional forms of political affiliation.[34]

This interest in sport had some interesting commercial side effects. Along with Western sport came
Western sporting goods. In 1975 the Kenya Olympic
Committee signed a contract with "Adidas" which would
have forced every Kenyan Olympian to wear equipment
made by that company. Kenyan track and field athletes
threatened to boycott the 1976 Olympics if such an agreement went into force. Kenyan presence in the Games was
felt to be too great an asset to lose, and the
government-controlled Olympic committee backed down.[35]

African countries also began to draw attention to
themselves by hosting international sporting events.
Dick Tiger, a Nigerian boxer, defeated Gene Fullmer for
the World Middleweight title in Nigeria. The bout's
location had resulted from a clamor on the part of
Tiger's fellow Ibos to hold the fight where they could
see it. The federal government, anxious to find a way
to maintain Ibo loyalty shortly before the "Biafra"
challenge, guaranteed the fighters and promoters $280,000
in order to do so.[36]

President Mobutu of Zaire needed no such prodding
to bankroll the fight between George Foreman and Muhammad
Ali in 1974. However, he did need a great deal more
money. The Zaire government spent a reported $49 million
on the fight, much of which reportedly went to civic
improvements designed to present a favorable image of
Kinshasha to the world.[37] The financial loss was
considered worth it, as long as it helped to turn the
country's 200 ethnic groups into "one great Zaire."[38]

There is a still more prestigious event worth holding for any state interested in its political prestige.
In 1968 the head of the Kenyan delegation at the Mexico
Olympics expressed an interest in bringing the 1976
Games to Nairobi.[39] It should not be surprising if
Kenya, Zaire, or another African state decides to use
the political prestige of hosting the Games to enhance
its international image, no matter what the cost (assuming that the IOC does not soon choose a permanent Olympic
site).

SOUTH AFRICA

Black Africa has provided the prototype for the use
of sport in a long-term diplomatic campaign. The
struggle to isolate South Africa in international sport
has been the single most extensive use of sport as an
instrument of diplomatic and political sanction. It
has also been a very effective form of attack against
the white supremacist regimes in Rhodesia and South
Africa.

As a political forum, the international sport
system is a natural place for such a campaign. Athletes
represent their states; to ignore them is to snub the
state. South Africa has been an especially good target
for such an attack, since it is among the most sport
conscious countries in the world.

South Africans participated in the earliest Olympiads, with Boers and English-speaking South Africans
using those Games as an expression of national identity
during and after the Boer War. South African sport
tradition thus antedated the policy of explicit Apartheid, which only grew up with National Party rule. In
the 1930's there was much contact between athletes of
different races, particularly in English-speaking areas.
Only in June 1956 was a law passed requiring an end to
inter-racial sport. When the International Table Tennis
Federation reacted by reiterating its ban on the all-
white South African Table Tennis Union, Interior Minister
Donges spelled out his government's policy:[40]

(1) White and non-white athletes must be
     separately organized.

(2) No mixed sport is allowed in South Africa.

(3) No mixed teams should be sent abroad.

(4) No mixed teams should visit from abroad.

(5) Non-whites from abroad can play South
     African non-whites.

(6) Non-white South African sport organizations
     must seek recognition through white organiza-
     tions (both internally and internationally).

(7) The government can refuse travel visas to
     those who would leave the country and then
     campaign against the presence of South
     Africa in international sport.

This policy not only reversed the previous tradition of mixed sport, but also explicitly linked South African sport to the social and racial policies of the regime. This was a political policy which utilized the Olympic Movement and its component parts (especially through point 6). The people who organized the opposition to South Africa in international sport were not creating an "intrusion" of politics. They were making a political answer to athletic apartheid, a policy thriving on Olympic institutions.

Sport Apartheid soon became a policy of consistent racial discrimination overtly based on the political doctrine of the South African regime. The political nature of the Olympic movement made South African participation in international sport a specific affirmation of Pretoria's legitimacy. It should not have been surprising, therefore, that opposition to South African sport soon began to grow, both inside the country and within its newly independent neighbors. The South African Sport Association (SASA) concentrated on getting non-racial sport institutions set up in South Africa while the South African Non-Racial Olympic Committee (SANROC) set up international institutions and challenged the all-white South African presence in international sport. This campaign was carried on in many sports and against many bilateral exchanges as well as in the Olympic Games.[41] Its success is only in part due to genuine concern with Apartheid.

The peripheral nature of political sport made it the easiest route for expressing displeasure with South Africa. In the 1960s, with increasing pressure upon many governments to ensure the rights of their own racial minorities, regimes used opposition to South African sport both to underscore commitments to "civil rights" and to deflect some of the pressure put on them to break more crucial political and economic ties with Pretoria. Governments could favor (or accept) an end to sport ties with South Africa without fear of political reprisal. Public demonstration of opposition to Apartheid could be made without necessitating an end to diplomatic or ecoomic ties with South Africa. Even now a state like Mozambique, for example, can retain ideological purity in sport organizations without altering its policy of permitting Mozambican citizens to work in South Africa.

By 1964, under such circumstances, South Africa had been ousted from the Olympic Games and from the competitions of several sport federations as well, despite repeated efforts by Avery Brundage and other Olympic officials to keep South African federations

active within the Olympic movement. The IOC constantly
tried to help Pretoria's position, only to be thwarted
by the South African assumption that given IOC support,
no concessions were necessary.

South Africa complicated its difficulties by
leaving the British Commonwealth in 1961. It soon found
itself isolated from Commonwealth states. Pretoria had
to arrange sport exchanges on an ad hoc basis, allowing
boycott advocates to concentrate on individual events
rather than having to spread their resources thin
attacking organizational legitimacy.

The IOC continued to help South Africa, despite
increasing pressure from the increasing number of third
world states in the Olympic system. Indeed, the only
reason that the IOC went along with South Africa's
expulsion from Tokyo (representation on that body was
still skewed in favor of traditional Olympic members)
was that Pretoria refused to go along even with half-
hearted IOC attempts to achieve some sort of movement
toward permitting non-white athletic participation on
South African teams.

In 1963 the IOC meeting scheduled for Nairobi had
to be moved to West Germany because the Kenyans would
not allow South Africa or Portugal (still in possession
of African colonies) to send all-white delegations.[42]
At this meeting the IOC issued an interesting warning:
"No discrimination is allowed against any country or
person on grounds of race, religion, or political
affiliation."[43] This warning's effect was diluted by
its wording. The IOC not merely attacked individual
discrimination, but political discrimination against
states as well. South Africa was thus warned to reform,
but led to believe that no action would be taken against
it if it did not. South Africa could claim, in future
years, that it was being discriminated against on the
grounds of its political policies.

So Pretoria held firm. In June 1964, the South
African government reiterated that it would not send
any mixed teams abroad and would not allow any to visit.
Somewhat to Pretoria's surprise, South Africa was then
barred from the 1964 Olympics.[44]

In this atmosphere the offensive against South
Africa became more intense. After Tokyo the South
Africans were in a more difficult situation than before
because they were on the outside trying to get back in.
South Africa could see that it would not be reinstated
unless at least token changes in its sport policy were
forthcoming. Black Africa, meanwhile, felt stronger
than ever. Strong African athletic performance in Tokyo
led to an increase in the use of sport throughout the

continent. The first All-African Games were held in
Brazzaville in July 1965. An organization was created
to institutionalize this event, since held at four-year
intervals.

In 1966 Dennis Brutus, a South African leader in the
anti-Apartheid struggle, founded the Supreme Council for
Sport in Africa, which began to coordinate the various
movements against South African sport. Success in
achieving South African explusion from several more
federations served as a prelude to Mexico City, by which
time the IOC hoped that Pretoria would agree to specific
IOC conditions in order to ensure its return to the
Olympic fold. Lord Killanin, then IOC Vice-President,
announced in 1967 that Pretoria promised to come up with
a single Olympic team of mixed racial make-up (at one
point South Africa had toyed with the idea of sending
separate white and non-white teams). All South African
Olympic athletes would wear the same colors and would
travel together. This team would be selected by a
board consisting of members of different races, and the
athletes would compete against each other at the Games.[45]
Killanin's colleagues, at their 1967 Tehran meeting,
then ordered South Africa to create a non-racial Olympic
committee (SANROC was not given consideration).

In February 1968, satisfied with South African
compliance, the IOC readmitted that state to the Olympic
Games, sparking a new round of boycott threats. This
movement was more complex and fractionalized than the
successful 1964 campaign since it involved issues other
than South Africa, specifically Rhodesia and American
blacks. In addition, black Africa had to weigh the
importance of Olympic success against the goal of
isolating South Africa. Boycott leaders were torn
between the desire of African states to show off their
physical prowess and the perceived necessity to oppose
Apartheid. Some black African athletes themselves were
quoted as being against the boycott.[46] As this problem
spilled over beyond the African context the Soviet
Union and United States tried to walk a verbal tightrope
between the two positions. The Soviets made many verbal
boycott threats, but at no time joined the boycott
itself.[47] Washington tried to balance opposition to
Apartheid, support for the separation of sport and
politics, and concern for the threatened black American
boycott. The boycott did finally hang together under
Kenyan leadership and both South Africa and Rhodesia were
kept out of Mexico.

In the period of 1968-1970 South Africa was forced
out of much of international sport. Kenya, still the
leader of the movement against South Africa among African
states, announced that its much sought-after runners

would boycott any British athletes who competed in the
1969 (all-white) South African Games.[48] This latter
competition became the focus of a South African attempt
to demonstrate that, despite its Olympic ouster, it still
possessed significant athletic legitimacy. Americans,
Europeans, and Australians were invited under the clear
understanding that the meet would be segregated. According to Peter Hain, Shell Oil provided much of the
financing.[49]

The results were mixed. West Germany pulled out
when African countries threatened to boycott the 1972
Munich Olympics.[50] The British straddled the fence; they
did not send an official team to the Games but did not
stop individual athletes from going on their own.

In other sports there were even more definitive
answers to UN Secretary-General U Thant's call for an
end to sport relations with South Africa.[51] Between
1968 and 1970, Pretoria was suspended from boxing, judo,
pentathalon, and weightlifting federations and was barred
from representation at the 1970 World Gymnastics Championships. While, for the time being, South Africa could
still send a team to Davis Cup tennis matches, some
states began to boycott rather than play them. Whenever
a South African team did show up it was greeted by
demonstrations and, at times, by violence.

The issue of South Africa reached its climax at a
1970 meeting of the IOC in Australia. Not only was South
Africa barred from the 1972 Olympics, but was also
expelled from the Olympic Movement as a whole. The
35-28-3 vote shows how the IOC was still slanted in favor
of traditional Olympic powers; 68 percent of the white
delegations voted for South Africa while 98 percent of
the non-whites voted against it.[52]

Between this meeting and the 1972 Games South Africa
reacted with a further show of intransigence. Prime
Minister Vorster reiterated that "no mixed sport between
whites and non-whites will be practiced locally."[53]
Despite prior elevation of Japanese businessmen to
"honorary white" status, the government kept a Japanese
jockey from entering the country.[54] Even Rhodesia was
expected to keep in line. A Rhodesian rugby team was
barred from South Africa because it included a member
of Chinese extraction.[55]

With South Africa out of the Olympic Movement, the
only racial question left on the agenda involved
Rhodesia. Salisbury's 1965 Unilateral Declaration of
Independence (UDI) was met by third world efforts to
ensure that Rhodesia would be as isolated as South
Africa in international sport. British opposition to
UDI and the precedent of the anti-South African struggle
made opposition to Rhodesia easy to galvanize. The
British position was clearly more important in IOC

discussion than African concerns. The main reason for
Rhodesia's ouster from the 1968 Olympics was the refusal
of the IOC to recognize its independent status.

Olympic officials, like many governments and
international organizations, continued to view Rhodesia
as a British colony. In September 1971 the IOC ruled
that Rhodesia could send a team to Munich as British
subjects.[56] Black Africa, once more led by Kenya,
threatened to boycott any Rhodesian presence.

IOC President Brundage pushed hard for a final
victory over "politics" before his retirement at the
Munich Olympics. He spoke out in favor of Rhodesian
participation, still believing that the movement against
that country was motivated by concerns irrelevent to
Olympic organization. His position was untenable in
view of the large number of states, and Olympic committees, either against Rhodesia or unwilling to buck
a boycott movement. Rhodesia was ousted from Munich,
an act which Brundage chose to consider as savage an
attack on the Games as the Palestinian assault on the
Israeli team.[57]

Rhodesia has since turned into Zimbabwe and re-
entered the Olympic fold. South Africa, meanwhile, has
been ostracized from nearly all of international sport.
Pretoria remains extremely sensitive to this type of
isolation; while it has continued to stand fast against
reforms in most areas of social life, it has made mixed
sport legal once more. South Africa has begun to publicize the exploits of its black athletes, portraying them
as discriminated against by the international sport system. Black athletes such as Arthur Ashe, Bob Foster, and
George Foreman have gone to visit South Africa; Ashe in
particular has campaigned for an end to South Africa's
athletic exclusion on the grounds that sport reforms can
become the basis for general societal change.[58]

This raises a serious question. Should black
athletes go to South Africa in order to provide a model
for non-white youth, or should they eschew all contact
with Pretoria in order to protest Apartheid's existence?
Each athlete must answer this for him or herself. It is
clear, however, that South Africa uses mixed sport to
provide a public distraction from Apartheid. The
government hopes that bi-racial rugby teams and mixed
tennis matches will make the sort of favorable impression
that counts for more among the mass audience of sport
than does the "homeland" policy which institutionalizes
the separation of the races in Southern Africa. This
use of sport has provided a means for the South African
government to appeal to North American and European
publicists whose favor might some day permit South
Africa to hope for at least partial readmittance to the
international athletic system.

ISRAEL

Unlike the Southern African problem, the Middle East situation has just begun to reach its full potential in sport. Neither the Arabs nor Israelis were original members of the Olympic Movement and until recently neither had a great deal of interest in the Games.

The ancient Olympics were, in fact, a challenge to the ancient Jews. Greek sport festivals were used by Hellenistic conquerers to lure Jews away from their own observances and rituals. There was some Zionist interest in modern sport; "Maccabiads" were held in the new city of Tel Aviv to advertise Israel to its future citizens and, in 1936, to draw some attention away from the Berlin Olympics. Israeli statehood brought with it creation of a national Olympic committee as one of the trappings of independence.

There was no Arab "Palestinian" Olympic Committee created to counter the political claims of Israel to sport legitimacy at the end of the British mandate, just as there was little interest expressed in a separate "Palestinian" Arab state in the early postwar period. The "Palestine" Olympic Committee, which existed in the interwar period under the British flag, became defunct when the area was left to itself.

Israel declared its independence in May 1948, and Israeli athletes tried to compete in London that summer (due to the climate of the region, this political sport contest has taken place almost exclusively in summer sporting events). The Arab states threatened to boycott if Israel was allowed in, but still did not create a Palestinian Olympic entity to oppose it. Since, to the IOC, it was not clear that there was any Olympic committee representing the area, and since the war to determine who would rule Palestine was just under way, the IOC chose to wait for a political victor and turned the Israelis away from London.

Israel considered trying to enter the Oslo winter Olympics in 1952, but lack of winter athletes and strong Arab pressure led it to concentrate on the Helsinki summer celebration. At that time an agreement existed on both sides of the Cold War that Israel had a right to exist. Stalin had supported Israel in its infancy; in 1952 he was just beginning to alter this policy. In addition, there was still no rival Arab Olympic body representing "Palestine." Israel was admitted to the Helsinki Games and Egypt, facing global acceptance of the Jewish state, withdrew its threat to boycott. The 1952 Olympics were one of the earliest international events, outside UN General Assembly sessions, attended by both Israelis and Arabs.

Several Arab states pulled out of the Melbourne Olympics because of the Suez Crisis, but this was directed against Britain and France as much as against Israel. In 1960 the Arabs were back in the Games and have not boycotted them since. Interestingly, no campaign for "Palestine" accompanied Indonesia's refusal to admit an Israeli team to the Fourth Asian Games in 1962 and no invitation was extended by Sukarno to "Palestine" to join the Games of the Newly Emerging Forces, held in Djakarta the following year.

After the 1967 War, however, Palestinian claims did coalesce into an international campaign to achieve recognition of their right to separate political existence. Terrorists, seeking the most direct method of attracting attention to their desires, sneaked into the Olympic Village at the 1972 Munich Olympics and murdered 11 Israeli athletes and coaches after having held them for several hours. Arab delegations, afraid for their own safety in an emotional hotbed, quietly left the Games.[59] The scene of Jews being killed in Germany partially destroyed the image of the new, friendly Germany so carefully built up in Olympic preparation.

The attack was the most deplorable event ever carried off at an Olympiad; it was an "intrusion" on the Games just as it would be in any part of the international political system, e.g., if the assault had come in a bus station or airport. It was, however, a comprehensible phenomenon in terms of the political content of the Olympic system, not an attack made especially heinous by its violation of Olympic soil.

As with any state, Israel's legitimacy is celebrated every time its athletes march in an opening Olympic ceremony. Palestinians chose an accessible public forum for the demonstration of their opposition to the existence of Israel and of their own determination to achieve their political goals. Such terrorism comes as a shock, of course, but should not be a surprise. As an expression of the political status quo the Games serve as a magnet for all forms of political demonstration against any existing state.

Recently the Arab campaign against Israel has expanded into many sports, particularly involving events with hosts friendly to the Arab cause. In 1975 India refused to issue visas to the Israeli team sent to the World Table Tennis Championships in Calcutta. A group from "Palestine-Gaza," on the other hand, was allowed to attend.[60]

Israel was barred from the 1978 World Karate Championships, the 1978 Asian Games, and the 1978 Asian Track and Field Championships on the grounds that security would be too costly in the wake of the Munich Olympics

and of the money spent in Montreal to prevent a recur-
rance of the killings. No Palestinian teams were noted
at these events, just as there was no significant effort
to put together a Palestinian team to challenge Israel
for the 1980 Olympics, an event deserving separate
treatment because of the unusual position of the host.

NOTES

1. Arthur E. Grix, Japans Sport in Bid und Wort
(Berlin: Wilhelm Limpert Verlag, 1937), p. 55.
2. Sports Illustrated, VIII, #8 (March 3, 1958),
pp. 56-64.
3. Sports Illustrated, IV, #12 (March 19, 1956),
p. 8.
4. Sports Illustrated, VIII, #7 (February
24, 1958), p. 61.
5. Swanpo Sie, "The Place of Health Education,
Physical Education, and Sport in Educational Planning
for National Development in Indonesia," (Ph.D. dissertation, University of Missouri-Columbia, 1971), p. 76.
6. Ibid., pp. 84-85.
7. Ewa T. Pauker, GANEFO I: Sports and Politics
in Djakarta (Santa Monica, Cal.: RAND, 1974), p. 4.
8. Ibid., pp. 16-17.
9. Tarasov, Soviet Sport Today, pp. 38-42.
10. Pauker, GANEFO I, p. 8.
11. Kolatch, Sports Politics, and Ideology in
China, pp. 189-201.
12. Pauker, GANEFO I, p. 3.
13. Kolatch, Sports, Politics, and Ideology in
China, p. 197.
14. China Sport, January, 1964.
15. China Sport, November 1965, p. 38.
16. Sports Illustrated, XXIV, #11 (March 14, 1966),
p. 11.
17. Richard Espy, The Politics of the Olympic Games
(Berkeley: University of California Press, 1979), pp.
139-141.
18. New York Times, August 8, 1936.
19. Michael Smith, Stanley Parker, and Cyril Smith,
Leisure and Society in Britain (London: Allen Lane,
1973), p. 220.
20. Sports Illustrated, XXVII, #23 (December
4, 1967), p. 17.
21. Sports Illustrated, XVII, #9 (August 27, 1962),
pp. 9-11.
22. Sports Illustrated, XVIII, #16 (May 6, 1963),
p. 10.
23. Sports Illustrated, XVII, #16 (October
5, 1962), p. 15.

24. *Sports Illustrated*, XXXII, #18 (February 23, 1970), pp. 13-14.

25. *New York Times*, December 17, 1974.

26. *New York Times*, April 16, 1975.

27. *New York Times*, May 9, 1975.

28. *New York Times*, May 11, 1975.

29. Richard Lapchick, "The Politics of Race and International Sport: The Case of South Africa" (Ph.D. dissertation, University of Denver, 1973), p. 225.

30. James Coote, *Olympic Report, 1968: Mexico and Grenoble* (London: Robert Hale, 1968), p. 22.

31. *Sports Illustrated*, XXIX, #4 (July 29, 1968), p. 9.

32. *Sports Illustrated*, XXII, #15 (April 12, 1965), p. 86.

33. *Sports Illustrated*, XXIX, #20 (November 11, 1968), p. 14.

34. Sidney Hall, "The Role of Physical Education and Sport in the Nation-Building Process in Kenya" (Ph.D. dissertation, Ohio State University, 1973), p. 223.

35. *New York Times*, April 22, 1975, April 23, 1975.

36. *Sports Illustrated*, XIX, #8 (August 19, 1963), pp. 12-18.

37. *New York Times*, January 7. 1975.

38. *New York Times*, August 18, 1974.

39. Hall, "The Role...Kenya," p. 244.

40. Lapchick, "The Politics of Race and International Sport," pp. 36-37.

41. See Lapchick, passim.

42. *Ibid*, p. 116.

43. Christopher Bracher, *Mexico, 1968* (London: Stanley Paul, 1968), p. 1.

44. Peter Hain, *Don't Play With Apartheid* (George Alle and Unwin, 1971), p. 35.

45. Goodhart and Chataway, *War Without Weapons*, p. 124.

46. *Sports Illustrated*, XXVIII, #33 (June 3, 1968), pp. 60-62.

47. Harry Edwards, *The Revolt of the Black Athlete* (New York: Free Press, 1969), pp. 135-136.

48. Hain, *Don't Play With Apartheid*, p. 101.

49. *Ibid*., p. 68.

50. *Sports Illustrated*, XXX, #13 (March 3, 1969), p. 6.

51. Lapchick, *The Politics of Race and International Sport*, p. 270.

52. *Ibid*., p. 368.

53. *Sports Illustrated*, XXXIII, #13 (September 28, 1970), p. 13.

54. Hain, *Don't Play With Apartheid*, p. 72.

55. *New York Times*, May 25, 1970.

56. _Sports Illustrated_, XXXIII, #9 (August 28, 1972), p. 35.

57. _Olympic Review_, #62-63 (January-February, 1973), pp. 16-18.

58. See David B. Kanin, "The Role of Sport in International Relations" (Ph.D. dissertation, Fletcher School, Tufts University, 1976), pp. 259-261.

59. _New York Times_, September 6, 1972.

60. _New York Times_, January 15, 1975.

7

The Moscow Olympics

The 1980 Olympic boycott was the most extensive diplomatic effort ever connected with an Olympic celebration. In view of this, and because of my own access to most of the traffic connected with the Moscow Olympics, I will deal with the 1980 Games in more detail than its predecessors. Of course, no classified information is used in the following analysis.

First, a disclaimer. By virtue of my interest in the politics of sport, I was on the margins of the process involved in US boycott policy regarding the 1980 Olympics. I served as a resource person for information on the Olympic Movement, its history, and its institutions. I had nothing to do with selling the boycott idea itself, or in formulating policies designed to implement it. I generally agreed with the purpose of the Olympic boycott, but had no influence over the means by which the administration attempted to give it life.

Before dealing with the boycott issue itself, loose ends in Olympic politics need to be tied up. The 1980 Olympic Games would have had significant political content even if Soviet troops had not invaded Afghanistan. Old issues in political sport remained, and new ones were emerging.

CREDENTIALS

The USSR promised to allow teams to enter the 1980 Olympics from all states with international Olympic recognition. This guarantee was made in reaction to Canada's refusal to permit athletes from Taiwan to attend the 1976 Games using passports reading "Republic of China." This problem lingered as the Lake Placid and Moscow Games approached, but in a different political context.

On the surface, the USSR faced the same situation
as had Canada; the Olympic host did not have diplomatic
relations with Taiwan. In addition, the Soviets had
spent the past quarter century posing as the spokesmen
for Peking's claims to Olympic recognition. To allow a
team from Taiwan, and not Beijing, into Moscow would
have been more than a change of policy; it would have
provided a spectacle of the world's first Socialist
Olympics without the world's most populous communist
state. Such an event would not only have demonstrated
continued Sino-Soviet animosity, it would have served
as a reminder to Beijing of its continued isolation
from certain areas of international relations. The
Soviets never did manage to convene an international
conference of communist parties to expel the Chinese
Communist Party. Olympic isolation could be publicized
as a partial substitute.

Relations between China and the Soviet Union were
never completely cordial. When Mao traveled to Moscow
after his victory over the Kuomintang, he was greeted
by Stalin as just another representative of a foreign
country, rather than as a victorious communist brother.
The recently abrogated Sino-Soviet Friendship Treaty of
1950 left Soviet troops in occupation zones in China,
and included a loan which the Chinese were expected to
repay with interest--two items Mao had not counted on.
Stalin's cool attitude toward his huge neighbor was
reflected in 1951. A Soviet basketball team traveled
to China and became the cause of a series of complaints
from Beijing to Moscow. The Soviet team insisted on
bringing its own ball (which the Chinese considered too
heavy), its own referee, and on changing the rules of
play.[1]

Despite this, most Soviet-Chinese athletic exchanges
of the 1950's were held in a friendly atmosphere. The
Chinese would often picture themselves as "learning"
from their Soviet comrades. Slowly, however, this did
begin to change. A 1962 description of a "friendly"
volleyball match pictured the Soviets as aggressive
attackers, and the Chinese as skillful defenders.[2] The
action was described as "fierce fighting over the net."

By 1964 the People's Republic was using sport to
underscore differences in the communist camp. A military
sport meet, held in China that year, featured the flags
of the participants on display. Those singled out for
attention at the meet included Albania, Poland, Romania,
Mongolia, North Korea, and North Vietnam.[3] At that time,
with the exception of Mongolia--a neighbor with which the
Chinese would like to have some influence--each of these
states was either allied with China, neutral in the dispute, or under the impression that it could mediate
between the communist giants.

In 1965 the split was openly advertised at a table tennis match between Soviet and Chinese teams. The match was held up almost forty minutes over a vehement Soviet protest against a type of serve used by their opponents.[4] Since 1965, with the Great Proletarian Cultural Revolution and China's slow recovery from it, there has been little in the way of Sino-Soviet sport.

Recent Chinese political initiatives made it more likely than at any time since 1956 that the mainland would be represented in an Olympic Games. China applied officially to rejoin the Olympic Movement in 1975. Neither this nor "Ping-Pong Diplomacy" originally made much of a difference in China's international sporting position. Only with the death of Mao, the expulsion of the Gang of Four, and the resulting reestablishment of diplomatic relations with the United States did Chinese athletic diplomacy threaten Taiwan's position on the IOC. The last event especially put Taiwan in a position of great isolation, removing its final tie to the political mainstream and to its Olympic component.

In addition, China changed its policy toward Taiwan's position at international sporting events. Beijing did not move to a "two-China" policy, but did attempt to absorb Taiwanese sports personnel into Chinese sport teams. In 1978 and 1979 there were several Chinese invitations to Taiwan sport federations to send teams to the mainland or join a Chinese delegation to an international event.

In 1979, encouraged by this attitude and by the US-China rapprochement, the IOC once more tried to arrange for two-China representation at the Olympics. Lord Killanin, IOC President and long-time supporter of mainland Chinese participation in the Olympics invited both Chinas to send delegations to Lausanne to discuss the situation. Both complied, although the Taiwanese were reluctant to do so. The latter hoped to speak to Killanin alone; they would not meet with Beijing's people, who further infuriated Taiwan by repeating an offer to form a joint team.

In April 1979, the IOC announced that a method had been found to bring teams from both governments to Moscow. Both delegations would represent "China," and would march separately in the opening ceremony. Their signs would read "Republic of China (Taipei)" and "People's Republic of China" or "Republic of China (Beijing)." The Taiwan government balked at the apparent deal, however, insisting on representation as "Chinese Taiwan Olympic Committee."[5]

While Taipei stalled settlement of the dispute, Beijing sweetened its case with a hint that it might offer to host the 1988 Olympic Games (that award is the least sought-after in years). The IOC, and

especially Killanin, finally decided to cut Taiwan off
once and for all. The IOC Executive Board convinced the
rest of the membership that only a team from the mainland could go to the Games unless Taipei accepted the
IOC's formula for admission. Rather than either giving
in or withdrawing from competition, Taiwan appealed the
IOC ruling in Swiss courts. The latter refused to get
involved in the politics of a "private" international
organization. Taiwan still sent athletes to Lake Placid,
and appealed its case to New York state courts, but to
no avail. The People's Republic of China competed as
the only China in the 1980 Winter Olympics and seemed
certain to do the same in Moscow.

Interestingly, the Soviets did not deviate from
their longstanding position of supporting Beijing's
claim, at least in public. They reportedly favored the
mainland at the 1979 IOC talks.[6] Nevertheless, Beijing
often claimed that the Soviets intended to invite Taiwan
to send a team to the 1980 Olympics.

To have a Chinese team in Moscow, of course, would
have complicated Soviet preparations. The presence of
Chinese athletes would have provided the most public contact between the two sides since the Ussuri border
clashes in 1969. The interplay of Chinese and Soviet
athletes in 1980 would have been a fascinating international event.

With the death of Mao, and even in the wake of the
Sino-Vietnamese-Kampuchean War, it is not clear that
future Sino-Soviet sport confrontations will be
entirely unfriendly. Although "Friendship First,
Competition Second" is a slogan presently in disrepute,
it could be put into practice to reflect a more correct
Sino-Soviet relationship. There would be no need to
end interparty polemics. Simple state-to-state contacts
would suffice (along with continued rehabilitation of
such comrades as the late Lo Juijing). A friendly
athletic show would be the most public way in which the
two sides could demonstrate a change in their public
postures.

The beauty of such a version of "Ping-Pong
Diplomacy" is that it does not have to mean anything.
Sport is a political process based on play, game, and
posture. Not only is the activity not serious, neither
are the positions of the national players. If Soviet and
Chinese athletes hold hands and dance around a stadium,
the world can be given a perception of better relations
without either side really making any concessions on the
difficult issues still dividing them. Under this
scenario, the 1980 Olympics would have started a three-
cornered "detente" in which no party would know quite
where it stands with the other two.

Of course, such contacts could go the other way as well. The Chinese could act coldly toward the Soviets, just as the latter did toward their American counterparts in Helsinki. Clearly the potential for political action is varied, in addition, by participation of other teams whose relationships with the Soviets are less than fraternal. In international events the Chinese can fraternize conspicuously with such Soviet rivals as Yugoslav basketball players, Romanian gymnasts, and Hungarian water polo players, thus extending the Chinese policy of seeking to take advantage of rifts in the Soviet camp.

This speculation will have to wait for another event in political sport. Beijing reacted cautiously to initial US expressions of interest in an Olympic boycott because, like other countries, China waited for Washington to make its position clear. It is interesting that Beijing did not take the lead in pushing for a boycott. The Chinese may have looked forward to celebrating the isolation of Taiwan in international sport, or they may have been wary of insulting an Olympic system which had just welcomed them in. In any case, with Taiwan safely out of the competition for the national mantle,[7] Beijing could make its boycott decision without worrying about the old legitimacy question. No "China" competed at the 1980 Olympic Games.

Another matter of recognition involved Israel. This issue was complicated by the question of Soviet Jewish dissidents, and by identification of some Soviet Jews with Israeli athletes in a fashion that resulted in a riot at the 1973 World University Games (Soviet Jewish fans were dragged from an arena after having rooted for an Israeli basketball team).

Before the boycott question loomed, it appeared doubtful that the Soviets could throw the Israelis out, at least under IOC guidelines. Some Arab interest was expressed in expelling Tel Aviv from the Olympic Movement federation by federation, but this idea bogged down due to lack of interest in some federations and outright failure in others.

Israel, in fact, even began to reverse some of its losses. North Korea, one of the staunchest supporters of the 1962 and 1978 Israeli expulsion from the Asian Games, invited an Israeli team to attend the 1979 World Table Tennis Championships in Pyongyang. The invitation eventually was withdrawan after intense Arab pressure, but it was noteworthy as an expression of interest in cultural relations between two countries considered very unlikely to have any.

A more promising approach was to bring up an old issue, one which would isolate Israel in sport and in world opinion. The Soviets led it be known that they

would keep out of the Games any state which retained
sport ties with South Africa. Israel, however, in a
gesture which showed how important it considered the
Games to be, temporarily broke off its ties with
Pretoria in January 1979. They shelved the idea, but
still damaged relations with one of Israel's few friends
in the world. The IOC, in a telling sidelight to this
affair, backed the Soviet position, and warned France
that a tour by the Springbok rugby team would result in
its expulsion from Moscow. The IOC, therefore, showed
that it now supported the position taken by the third
world states which boycotted the 1976 Olympics because
New Zealand would not cut its athletic ties to South
Africa.

The USSR remains in an ambiguous position regarding
Israel. It does not call for the destruction of Israel,
yet does conform to the view that Zionism equals racism.
Relations between the two are suspended, leaving a
diplomatic position similar to that between Taiwan and
the last two Olympic hosts. The politics of the issues
are not, however, exactly the same. If Galia Golan is
correct,[8] the USSR is committed to a policy pushing
eventual recognition of Israel--as a fact of life--by
the Arab states. Soviet acceptance of an Israeli
Olympic presence would have been a way of reinforcing
this policy in a public forum. Since sporting relations
involve only tacit diplomatic recognition, the Soviets
could have admitted Israeli Olympic athletes and still
have maintained an official policy opposing international Zionism. Once more, since the posture of sport does
not require a change in political policy, anti-Zionist
propaganda need not have been stopped.

In pre-Afghanistan Olympic preparations, it is
possible that some sort of Arab pressure would have been
put on Moscow to expel Israel. The Egyptian-Israeli
peace treaty was met by angry Arab reactions ranging
from terrorist attacks to demands that the oil weapon
be put into use against the West. The Arabs might have
decided to test Soviet loyalty by using the Olympic card
as well. In this vein, relations between Israeli and
Egyptian athletes on the one hand, and between Egyptian
and Arab athletes on the other, would have been an interesting sideshow in 1980. However, as with China, Israel
boycotted the Games reluctantly, putting solidarity with
the US position before the temptation to give Soviet Jews
a Jewish team to root for.

Israeli absence eased the way for a Soviet invitation to Yasser Arafat to attend the Games. The PLO
chief toured the Olympic Village eight years after the
attack in Munich on Israel's Olympic team, an attack the
PLO never condemned.

Still another credentials problem involved an old
Soviet wound. In early 1979, the USSR tried to arrange
for athletes from West Berlin to be somehow separate
from the West German team in Moscow. Bonn raised a storm
of protest, causing the Soviets to back down. The USSR
still is sensitive on this issue, having boycotted meets
held in the divided city under West German auspices as
recently as 1977. Moscow might next have tried a related
approach, involving the two Germanies themselves. Despite the existence, since 1968, of two German Olympic
presences, West Germany still calls itself "Germany,"
extending the fiction that it is the sole true representative of the German people (East Germany goes to the
Games as the "German Democratic Republic"). If the West
Germans had not boycotted the 1980 Olympics, it is
possible that the Soviets would have attempted to get
Bonn to send a team from "The Federal Republic of
Germany," in order to give its own German client political equity to go along with its athletic supremacy.
Finally, the choice of the Olympic yachting site
offered potentially contentious political content. The
West does not recognize the incorporation of Talinn,
the rest of Estonia, or of Latvia or Lithuania in the
USSR. The Soviets acquired these three countries as
part of the Hitler-Stalin Pact. Moscow sought Western
recognition of these gains by involving the US, West
Germany, and other states in the Talinn Olympic regatta.
Before Afghanistan there was no evidence of any Western
intention to boycott this event, although special
diplomatic gymnastics might have been considered.

THE OLYMPIC HOST

The 1980 Olympic Games were not only the first
Olympics awarded to a Socialist state; they were also
the first with a totalitarian host since 1936. The USSR
is "totalitarian" in that it seeks to control <u>every</u>
aspect of its citizens' social life. Leisure and recreation are as important to the Communist Party as production quotas and political education. Interpersonal
communication is made a delicate matter by state security
organs charged with the task of circumscribing its scope
and content.
The Soviets remembered that the 1959 Moscow World
Youth Festival had resulted in Soviet youth being
infected with Western ideas, and with the intellectual
roots of the contemporary dissident problem. The authorities recognized that the Olympics could once more open
Soviet society to a crush of Western reporters, fast-buck
artists (the Olympics gave the booming Soviet black
market a big boost) and assorted thrill-seekers. The
1980 Olympic Games, though relatively sparsely attended,

still opened up the USSR to the most outside scrutiny
in its history. For two weeks Moscow had to deal with a
few of the problems of open societies.

The Soviets had been preparing for their Olympic
problems since their capture of the 1980 award. Moscow
not merely had its streets cleaned; it systematically
removed its dissidents to accomodations not corresponding exactly to the Olympic village.* By arresting the
most famous of these individuals before the Games (the
process goes back at least to the Shcharansky trial in
1978) the Soviets hoped to bear the brunt of Western
criticism early enough for feelings to defuse should the
West have considered making an Olympic boycott a policy
alternative. Before Afghanistan, except for a few
American congressmen, this threat did not materialize.
The Soviets were able to arrest lesser known individuals
in an atmosphere of continually decreasing interest in
the West. Sakharov, of course, was another story.

Just in case not all uninvited persons could be
cleared from Olympic sites before the Games, the Soviets
covered their bets with a series of elaborate security
preparations. Some of this was couched in preparations
necessary for the prevention of incidents such as happened to the Israeli team in Munich in 1972. Other
aspects, however, reflected some of the special security
concerns of a closed society opening itself up to a
televised invasion.

A huge press center was one of the projects under
construction for the Games. Some American reporters
probably were surprised at the sophistication of this
ediface. It was in the Soviet interest to keep an-
nouncers hermetically sealed in an environment where
they could push buttons instead of roaming the streets
in search of troublemakers. Interestingly, when the
United States government temporarily stalled the deal
which sent a computer to TASS for the Games, the Soviets
were faced with having to find an alternative supplier
of a vital part of their preparations for Western
journalists.

Of course some reporters could have roamed the
stadium sidelines, perhaps even the stands. A repeat
of the 1973 World University Games incident for a
television audience might have proven embarrassing, but
this too was dealt with. The Soviets added a wrinkle
to the "fan club" concept. These organizations have a

---

*Amnesty International estimated that the Soviets
arrested or tried 144 dissidents between October 1979
and the July 1980 Olympic opening.[9] This, of course,
was only the final stage in this campaign.

restricted membership which got control over domestic
ticket sales. With a members only policy, anyone not
considered reliable could effectively be kept away from
the Games.

Despite these precautions, a few individuals managed to get through Soviet security and stage brief
demonstrations. Moscow arrested several reporters who
covered events not on the Olympic calender, and used
control over their press facilities to kill reports
filed by several more. France officially protested
Soviet treatment of French journalists covering the
Games.

For its part, the IOC did its best to help the
Olympic host. Lord Killanin urged reporters to cover
only sporting events. IOC officials, like athletes and
foreign tourists, were uncomfortable with stifling Soviet
security procedures, but restricted their protests to
anonymous asides to journalists. Track and field
officials, cornered by Soviet security, were slow even
to push their way on to the athletic field for the
purpose of checking disputed results in field events.

AFGHANISTAN

Other security issues came to dominate the Olympics.
As noted above, the idea of boycotting the 1980 Olympic
Games first came to public notice in 1978. The trial
of Anatoly Shcharansky, a scientist and a leading Soviet
Jewish dissident, aroused both Jewish groups and Helsinki
Act monitors. It was argued that the move against
Shcharansky was, in part, directed at Moscow's Olympic
problems. If indeed the Soviets were trying to make
Moscow antiseptically clean of dissidents before the
latter had a chance to contact Olympic visitors, some
felt that a boycott would be an appropriate means of
bringing life to US human rights policy. Since it would
be assumed that the Soviets were violating human rights
as a direct reaction to an international event, the
standard Soviet line that such things were purely of
domestic concern would seem weak.

A few congressmen and senators indeed argued for an
American reaction against the Moscow Olympics. They
anticipated the 1980 events by calling for the Games to
be moved, rather than boycotted. One of the weaknesses
of US policy throughout the Olympic issue was slowness
in understanding that moving or cancelling the Games
was very unlikely, and that the question always boiled
down to who would go to Moscow and who would not.

President Carter ruled out a boycott or other anti-
Olympic policy in 1978, and the issue would have been a
footnote somewhere in this essay had not the Soviet Union
invaded Afghanistan a few days after Christmas in 1979.

The Soviet claim that their troops simply responded to request for aid from a friendly government dissolved in the suspicious death of Hafizollah Amin, the head of that government, and his quick replacement by Babrak Karmal, who seemed to have reached power from the baggage of the Soviet army. The reasons usually advanced for the invasion, revolving around Soviet concern for the stability of their Moslem population, Soviet designs in the oil-rich Persian Gulf, and Moscow's commitment to preserve Communist regimes once they achieve power, all seem plausible. However, the actual calculus of the Soviet action remains unclear. The move might have been a message to East Europeans that their own regimes were in power to stay (a reinforcement of the Czechoslovakia lesson) or even simply an opportunity taken while the United States was paralyzed by events in neighboring Iran.

In any case, Soviet adversaries in Europe and the United States perceived Moscow to have crossed a new threshold by intervening in a state not considered part of their sphere of influence (despite the fact that a communist government had ruled in Kabul--if nowhere else in Afghanistan--since April 1978). While West Europeans compared the problem to Hungary and Czechoslovakia, the US felt frustrated and searched for ways to demonstrate how seriously it took this Soviet challenge.

So, in a way, Washington faced a situation similar to the Soviet dilemma over Vietnam. In both cases a superpower felt an urgent need to react to their adversary's actions without losing control of the ever-dangerous and barely balanced nuclear stalemate.

Sport, that most peripheral and most publicized form of international relations, provided the perfect answer. It is doubtful that the Soviets thought President Carter would indeed boycott the Olympics (and if he did, Afghanistan simply was more important than the Games). They probably knew that they could count on the IOC to hold to the Moscow award, and on the West to react to Afghanistan the way it reacted to Czechoslovakia (the major diplomatic efforts of the detente era flowered six months after that 1968 Soviet intervention).

It is important to keep in mind that the Olympic boycott was only one of the economic and political sanctions making up the US response to Afghanistan. The others, which included the grain embargo, restrictions on sales of high technology goods and processes, and curtailment of the whole gamut of scientific and cultural exchanges, involved issues more important to the Soviet economy, but did not provide the potential for public embarrassment the way the Olympics did. Without the US in Moscow the Games would turn into a large-scale Spartakiade, or a simple Soviet-East German dual meet. The Soviet populace might draw together in a patriotic reaction, but would also be aware of how seriously Afghanistan affected East-West relations. Any large-scale international support for the US move would add to the embarrassment, and reduce the political legitimacy the Soviets hoped to gain from hosting the Olympic spectacle.

The boycott idea evidently was under tentative consideration at the White House almost immediately after the Soviet invasion. The President seems to have been reluctant to use it, perhaps in line with his refusal to use the Olympic weapon over Shcharansky or because he assumed that most Americans would prefer to compete in Moscow. Press speculation began immediately, of course, and Vice-President Mondale floated the boycott idea while campaigning for the President in Iowa (the fact that Olympic years are also election years never was more obvious). Carter's first personal boycott hint came in his January 4 address to the country on Afghanistan and Iran. He insisted that he preferred to see a US team go to Moscow, but that the Soviets would have to realize that their actions made such participation questionable. Polls and statements from public figures soon indicated that a 1980 Olympic boycott, in contrast to the 1936 and 1978 precedents, was a popular idea. The public in general seemed to view a boycott as a vent to frustrations caused as much by apparent US impotence over Iran as by Soviet actions. Such powerful groups as the AFL-CIO intensified boycott pressure by resurrecting the Shcharansky issue.

The USOC and its supporters were put on the defensive by Afghanistan. Olympic officials tried to insist that politics should not interfere in sport, but this time few people believed the old mythology. Political sport finally had reached public consciousness, perhaps because of the problems in Munich and Montreal, or because of the obvious comparison with 1936. In any case, USOC arguments that the best way to fight Soviet aggression was to beat them on the playing fields fell on deaf ears.

The International Olympic Committee, of course, also used its traditional arguments concerning the sanctity of sport. Carter's appeals that the Games be moved were brushed aside, both for contractual reasons and because it was too late to alter the award. IOC Administrative Director Monique Berlioux issued veiled threats against the Los Angeles Olympic award, and the IOC refused to alter any of its preparations.[10] International athletic federations took the same line as the IOC. Lord Killanin, however, noted that no national Olympic committee had to send a team to Moscow.

US athletes themselves were strongly opposed to losing their chance at Olympic glory, but were as ineffective as the USOC in their appeals to public opinion. Some appeared selfish when they admitted both ignorance of the political situation and total focus on their individual efforts. Others expressed helplessness at a situation which they simply did not understand. Still others, such as three-time gold medal winner Al Oerter, insisted that, once the government made its decision, athletes would have to go along.

Interestingly, US amateur athletes failed to use the issue in their longstanding fight with USOC officials for control of US amateur sport. In neglecting the politics of sport, athletes long have been vulnerable to officials with a better understanding of political processes. If athletes had broken with their officials on the boycott question, they might have been able to convince a sympathetic congress to speed up stalled attempts to reform the amateur sport system. As it was, they failed either to stop the boycott or to increase their influence over their own activities.

When President Carter finally announced his decision to boycott the Games, assuming that Soviet troops still were in Afghanistan by February 20, the USOC announced that it would poll prospective Olympic athletes before making any decision on the issue. From that point until close to the May 24 deadline for Olympic invitation acceptance, the USOC stalled its own political process, hoping that somehow the Soviets would leave Afghanistan or public opinion would turn against boycott efforts. Throughout the next several months Olympic officials seemed off balance, embarrassed, and unsure what they would do.

In both his January Meet the Press statement and the subsequent State of the Union address, President Carter repeated his preference that the Games be moved or cancelled, rather than boycotted. In addition, he later rejected the idea that the Soviets be barred from competition at the Lake Placid winter Olympics. Carter tried to distinguish between an attack on the Olympic Movement and a refusal to take part in Soviet use of the Games to celebrate the assault on Afghanistan. In making this distinction, however, he also promised to search for alternative games that would ensure world-class competition for US athletes. The administration vastly underestimated the problems of these games, both in terms of getting logistic arrangements settled and in obtaining approval from international sport federations. The overwhelming vote at the February 11-12 Lake Placid IOC meeting against US proposals that the Olympics be moved (dutifully presented to the IOC by US Olympic officials) was accompanied by total rejection of the alternative games idea.

The US position faced other problems. Munich and Montreal refused to take the Olympic Games even if the IOC agreed to move them and Mexico showed outright hostility to American Olympic policy. In addition, the alternative games idea conjured up memories of GANEFO, hardly a comforting thought to Olympic decisionmakers.

The alternative games were doomed by a basic contradiction. No federation or natural Olympic committee would sanction an event that banned athletes who attended the Olympic Games. To permit athletes to participate in both events (as was eventually decided), on the other hand, would be to encourage governments to take the easy way out of the issue by making sure their athletes did so. In either case, the alternative games idea would not accomplish its basic purpose, reducing the number of national teams in Moscow.

They might accomplish a secondary purpose, however. The President, once having promised alternative games, chose to pursue them for the sake of mollifying American athletes. Meetings were held in Geneva in March to plan the events, and the administration continued to express optimism about the future of these games even though most countries, including West Germany, France, Italy, Japan, and other important allies, paid little attention to them. "Alternative games" deteriorated into "additional games," and the concept proved to be an insignificant part of the 1980 Olympic issue.

The concentration on alternative games distracted US officials from other strategies, such as approaches to individual federations designed to remove individual sports and components of national teams from Moscow. Partial boycotts, nevertheless, eventually played an important role in devaluing Olympic competition in several sports.

President Carter based his boycott formula on the contention that neither he, the Congress, nor the American people would tolerate a US Olympic presence in Moscow unless Soviet troops left Afghanistan within a month of his warning. February 20 became a deadline that the US was stuck with. It was an arbitrary position, one neither allowing much time for a South Asian settlement nor clearly showing athletes that, indeed, they would not be going to Moscow. As the deadline approached, apparently conflicting signals clouded the picture further. The White House seemed to indicate that a Soviet withdrawal between February 20 and May 24 still might allow an American Olympic presence. The State Department, on the other hand, insisted that the

February 20 deadline was final. This confusion permitted the USOC to delay its decision while the President and his advisors scrambled to convince Olympic officials that boycott policy was firm. Foreign leaders also did not know how to react. If they declared for a boycott and the US pulled back they would be greatly embarrassed, probably to the detriment of relations with both superpowers.

Administration confusion gave the USOC time to ride out boycott mementum and press for policy reversal. While US public opinion remained against Olympic participation, other countries seemed to hold back, causing USOC officials to claim that the US would be isolated in its boycott efforts. The late March British Olympic Association vote to defy Prime Minister Thatcher and attend the Games, while completely predictable, still fueled sentiment among US Olympic officials favoring an Olympic vote against the President and his "mixture" of sport and politics.

The administration responded to this revolt with simple political pressure. First, the President ordered stopped transfer of technology and goods meant for use in the Olympic effort. This included the final $20 million NBC owed to the Soviets. Next, the Secretaries of State and Defense insisted that an American Olympic presence would threaten national security, and personally appealed to Olympic officials' patriotism. Finally, the President himself repeated the national security theme, and coupled it with a threat to take legal action to stop American Olympic participation.

The USOC finally gave up on April 12, voting by a 2-1 margin for a boycott after a final plea from Vice-President Mondale. The athletes, meanwhile, planned lawsuits against their Olympic officials, never realizing that their single-minded intent to compete had cost them a chance to reform the system that, as always, brushed them aside.

Thus, there was no US presence in Moscow, save for a few thousand tourists and US citizens of dual nationality competing for other countries. As an anti-climax to the boycott, the IOC succumbed to US pressure and agreed to use the flag of the city of Los Angeles and the Olympic hymn instead of the US flag and national anthem in the ceremony by which the XXII Olympiad closed and the XXIII opened.

THE SOVIET POSITION

The Soviet Union, of course, deplored the American position. Since its Olympic literature claimed that the Olympic award was a vindication of Soviet policy and testimony of the natural rivalry between capitalism and socialism in sport, Moscow tried hard to ensure maximum Olympic participation. In general, the Soviets stressed (1) their desire to keep sport and politics separate, (2) Moscow's intention to adhere to Olympic rules and its contract with the IOC, (3) the futility of Washington's efforts to organize an Olympic boycott and alternative games and (4) that US policy resulted from the knowledge that the athletes of socialism would defeat those from the West. The Soviets initially were confident that few countries would boycott the Olympics, and hoped that even the US position was not set in concrete.

There is little question that the Soviet leadership was embarrassed by boycott efforts, but perhaps thought that the world would be impressed with a superpower that was willing to use force to achieve its aims even in the face of organized international condemnation. Rather than cut its losses, the Kremlin strongly defended its Afghan adventure and blamed US, Egyptian, Pakistani, and Chinese aid to ousted feudal classes as the cause of the problem in the first place. The Soviets also refuted the idea that Afghanistan threatened world peace, blaming global tension instead on US delay of SALT II ratification and on NATO's December 1979 decision to modernize its long-range theater nuclear forces.

As the Western reaction hardened, however, the Soviets took on the Olympic issue more directly. By the middle of March Moscow probably believed that the Americans would not be coming to the Games, since from that time Soviet attacks on the boycott issue included extremely harsh attacks on Carter and hints that an Olympic boycott might itself be a threat to overall East-West relations.[11]

Moscow asserted that the US, by denying its athletes a trip to the Olympics, was violating human rights principles. It is possible that Washington--which was preparing for human rights protests of its own--delayed forceful measures against its athletes partly to avoid human rights implications. Carter even noted his intention not to stop individual athletes from attending the Games (a safe statement considering Olympic rules).[12] It seemed probable that Moscow would make the Olympic boycott a human rights issue during the upcoming Madrid meeting of European states to review implementation of the 1975 Helsinki Final Act.

The East Europeans followed the Soviet line, showing fewer differences in nuance than over the Afghan issue generally. The Soviet satellites were not pleased with an invasion of Afghanistan that threatened the delicate relationship built with Western Europe since the Czechoslovakia crisis, but were less pleased still with

the prospect of a Western Olympic boycott that would
not only cut off a major point of contact with the West,
but might itself exacerbate the danger to detente posed
by the overall political atmosphere.

Even Romania--with its well-known opposition to
Soviet interventionism--supported Moscow's Olympic
position. Bucharest's main problem regarding the
Olympics was with the scores Soviet bloc gymnastic
judges gave Nadia Comanici. Romanian editorials attacked the judging of early events without, of course,
mentioning the Soviets by name.[13] This was not the
first time Romania had attacked Soviet gymnastics
judging, but it certainly was the most publicized.

The USSR, already hard pressed by the boycott, had
no desire for intra-bloc squabbles. It appears likely
that Soviet and East European judges eventually arranged
to divide gold medals among Warsaw Pact participants.
Both Moscow and Bucharest seemed basically satisified
with the final tally.[14]

Yugoslavia, not in the Soviet orbit and facing its
long-awaited succession crisis, was a special case. The
Olympic question was the last thing Belgrade needed in
an already tense situation, and it worried that a boycott in July might lead to scuttling of the November
meeting scheduled in Madrid for the purpose of reviewing
the Helsinki Final Act. Yugoslavia was one of a number
of states concerned that the Conference on Security and
Cooperation in Europe (CSCE), the outgrowth of the
Helsinki process and very important as long as SALT and
other security forums were stalled, might suffer as a
result of an Olympic debacle. Belgrade sent a team to
Moscow.

THE ALLIES

Western Europe, site of the theater nuclear force
decision and the major theater in the Soviet-American
relationship, was the center of the most intense lobby-
ing by both superpowers on the boycott issue, and the
focus of the vast majority of diplomatic efforts surrounding the Olympic question. While the West Europeans
were angered by Soviet actions, they did not believe
Afghanistan affected European security as much as overall superpower relations. Detente, therefore, could be
divisible.

The allies originally hoped for a South Asian
regional response to Soviet actions in cooperation with
other Moslem states. In short, the allies hoped the
issue would be more an East-South than an East-West
problem. The West Europeans did not feel that the US
had consulted with them adequately before embarking on

the sanctions route, and specifically found the
Olympic boycott not to their liking. President Carter
insisted that the United States would boycott alone if
necessary, but obviously hoped to garner as much international support as possible. Originally, none was
forthcoming from Western Europe, aside from Great
Britain, and even the British government could not be
sure of controlling its national Olympic committee.

The Soviets immediately exploited allied indecision,
noting that the United States' position was not to it.
allies' liking. As some allies began, reluctantly, to
move toward the American stance, Moscow portrayed these
allies as being forced away from the Olympics by the US,
rather than as acting in response to Soviet policy.[15]

National considerations among the West Europeans
were as follows:

Great Britain's Prime Minister Thatcher was the
most supportive of US sanctions and of the boycott idea
in particular. She urged her European colleagues to
follow the US lead. The Soviets assumed that the British
would boycott and soon singled them out for vilification.
As in the case of Saudi Arabia, the earliest boycott
adherent, the Olympic host sought to explain possible
British absence from the Games on grounds unrelated to
the actual political issues.

In 1979 the British had allowed a South African
rugby team to tour the United Kingdom, drawing the wrath
of the Supreme Council for Sport in Africa, which
demanded that the British be expelled from Moscow.[16]
If the British did not go the Olympics, according to
Izvestiya, this was the reason.[17]

The Soviets need not have bothered. Mrs. Thatcher's
appeal was met with overt hostility on the part of the
British Olympic Association (BOA) and its athletes.
The British sport establishment prided itself on being
the fount of international sport, and considered the
separation of sport and politics an English trust. On
January 21 the BOA insisted that its athletes would go
to Moscow regardless of the government's position.[18]

West Germany, however, was the key to both European
and non-European support for an Olympic boycott.
Bonn was particularly vulnerable on this issue; on the
one hand it wanted to show solidarity with the United
States, on the other it did not want to lose the
Ostpolitik that was the cornerstone of its foreign policy.
West Germany had great economic as well as political
stakes in improvement in East-West relations. In
addition, Ostpolitik was the basis for normalized relations with East Germany, the preeminent issue for all
Germans.

The Ostpolitik was the underpinning of Social-
Democratic Party (SPD) rule. 1980 was an election year
in West Germany as well as the United States, and both
Chancellor Schmidt and his opponents knew that security
policy would be a major political issue. Schmidt could
not win an argument with Franz-Josef Strauss, his
conservative opponent, on the subject of getting tough
with Moscow. Nevertheless, Schmidt had to do something
to satisfy both popular anger over Soviet actions and
American demands for Western coordination.

Predictably, the opposition immediately called for
West German adherence to an Olympic boycott. At the
same time, former Chancellor Willy Brandt and Egon Bahr,
the architects of Ostpolitik and on Schmidt's left in
the SPD, expressed contempt for the boycott idea. The
Frankfurter Rundeschau, a paper with ties to the SPD
left, warned that an Olympic boycott would have
"devastating" consequences for both East and West, and
would destroy the Olympic besides.[19]

Given such conflicting conditions, Schmidt's
caution on the issue was understandable. He probably
opposed a boycott personally and, before the Sakharov
affair, probably wound not have joined one. He made no
statements himself in the wake of Carter's call, leaving
it to parliamentary spokesmen and party officials to
construct an ambiguous, basically anti-boycott government position. The most definitive comment came from
Interior Minister Baum, who noted the difficulty of
getting independent sport officials to do government
bidding.[20] Baum ruled out government pressure in the
form of travel restrictions or financial squeezes.
Foreign Minister Genscher met with US Secretary of
State Vance on January 21, promising only to consult
the West German Olympic Committee.

Willi Daume, IOC member for West Germany and an IOC
vice-president, showed no such indecision. He led a
chorus of West European Olympic committee statements
insisting that European teams would go to Moscow. Daume,
Willi Weyer, Berthold Beitz, and other West German sport
officials recognized the important international position they held, and were determined to lead their
counterparts to the Games.

The French position seemed crystal clear. Paris
opposed sanctions that would turn a South Asian problem
into a European one. Paris only condemned the Soviet
invasion of Afghanistan after considerable domestic and
international prodding, and refused to join in a unified
Western response to it. France made its opposition to
a boycott clear; Sport Minister Soisson promised to permit French sporting authorities complete control over
the participation of their athletes in the Games.

In sum, the major West European allies either would not or could not support a boycott move. They hid behind their Olympic committees when necessary, deflecting US pressure with claims of impotence in influencing Olympic committee behavior. Only Mrs. Thatcher supported the President, and she also promised not to force anything on her athletes. For their part, national Olympic committees expressed disdain for the boycott. Significantly, however, none of them gave in to Soviet requests that they issue early acceptances of the Olympic invitation.

The boycott prognosis changed abruptly on January 22, when the USSR suddenly sentenced Andrei Sakharov to internal exile near Gorky. It is not clear why the Soviets made this move. Perhaps they felt that the Afghan crisis was so deep that nothing could make it worse. In 1978, after the Shcharansky trial, other dissidents were detained without arousing much interest in the West, and Moscow might have believed that, in the wake of Afghanistan, the West was similarly distracted. On the other hand, the Sakharov arrest may have been scheduled long before Afghanistan, as the culmination of a process of rounding up dissidents in time to prevent their contact with Olympic visitors.

If the Soviets believed that Afghanistan would distract the West from Sakharov they were badly mistaken. His arrest was far more of a shock to the West Europeans than Afghanistan, and it was the repression of the leading Soviet dissident that made West European support for an Olympic boycott possible, even though governments and Olympic committees continued to measure their positions by the Afghan problem.

Soviet dissidents themselves faced an interesting choice in attitudes toward the boycott question. They could welcome foreigners to Moscow by advertising their plight; the Olympics would provide Soviet dissidents with the greatest potential audience they would ever have. Dissidents could attempt to show a side of Soviet life never seen on television, provided that they could outwit the KGB. Their other alternative was to support a boycott, in the belief that the Olympics themselves were the reason for increased Soviet repression and because they knew that the regime would be publicly humiliated if many countries, or even just the United States, stayed away from the Games.

In November 1979, Vladimir Bukovsky, a leading dissident, urged the IOC to take the Olympics away from Moscow, terming a Soviet Olympic celebration a "betrayal" of human rights.[21] Alexander Ginzburg, who had originally supported Western presence at the Olympics, changed his mind in the wake of the Sakharov affair. Ginzburg,

Bukovsky, Andrei Amalrik, Leonid Plyusch, and other
prominent emigrees organized a Committee to Boycott the
Games on the day of Sakharov's internal exile.
Shcharansky's wife, Avital, also pushed for a boycott.

The move against Sakharov immediately pushed the
Olympic question to the forefront of suggested West
European sanctions against the USSR. Whereas Afghanistan was a crisis thousands of miles away, the human
rights question touched the heart of East-West relations.
The first reaction came from the Netherlands, where
Prime Minister Van Agt announced that he would advise his
athletes to boycott the Games.[22] The Dutch government
already had cut off funds from its Olympic effort, but
this alone had not been expected to prevent Dutch
Olympic participation. It was not clear that Van Agt's
statement would do so either.

Norway, another small country with a traditional
interest in human rights, became the first European
country in which the national Olympic committee voted
to boycott the Olympics. Soviet-Norwegian relations
already were at a low point over Norwegian consideration
of NATO request to increase its storage of NATO-related
supplies. Oslo's Olympic position made matters much
worse. The Soviet press launched a barrage of
vilification against Norwegian foreign policy. While
the Norwegian Olympic Committee reversed itself in
March, due to lack of support from other Olympic bodies,
Norwegian support for the US position remained probable.

An Olympic boycott now became conceivable to the
larger West European states, where the Sakharov affair
outraged governments and publics alike. The boycott
question was decided largely on the basis of domestic
political considerations, including public opinion
polls, the relationship between governments and national
Olympic committees, and estimates of the state of intra-
party relations. The United States made a serious error
in failing to stress Sakharov along with Afghanistan
in its boycott strategy.

West Germany remained the most influential country.
Polls showed the Sakharov affair to have made a boycott
popular. It was not clear how long such feeling would
last, and how deeply an Olympic boycott would affect
Soviet-West German relations. Bonn's state in Ostpolitik
remained great, but human rights considerations made it
very difficult for the West Germans to send a team to
Moscow. Schmidt now concentrated on lining up other
West Europeans for a common position, so that if a boycott did develop West Germany could keep as low a profile as possible.

Foreign Minister Genscher, head of the junior coalition partner Free Democratic Party (FDP), clearly was more disposed to a boycott than the Chancellor. Genscher, after a meeting with the Soviet ambassador in Bonn, affirmed that the Olympic Games were in "great danger" as a result of Soviet policy in South Asia.[23]

Government spokesmen continued to reflect caution, and denied that the Federal Republic had joined the boycott effort. On February 15 Schmidt, after a meeting with the Soviet ambassador, repeated his foreign minister's fears, but insisted that his policy had not yet been determined,[24] a position he repeated six days later.[25]

Genscher, however, soon went beyond his earlier statements, picking up the slogan that it was up to the Soviets to create conditions under which the Games would be held in Moscow (thus implying that those conditions did not presently exist). Genscher contended that West Germany, unlike France, was solidly behind the United States, and that the US could count on Bonn in support for Afghan policy. This formula fit in well with Ostpolitik, putting the onus for dangers to detente squarely on Moscow. Genscher thus disliked the word "boycott" preferring to view Soviet, not Western, actions as the cause of the Olympic problem.

Schmidt's early March visit to the United States produced mixed results. US officials insisted that the Chancellor had assured President Carter than West Germany would eventually join the boycott effort.[26] Schmidt went beyond the Genscher formula for his US audience, stating that conditions for West German Olympic participation "do not now" exist.[27]

On returning home, however, Schmidt restated his opinion that an Olympic boycott could have an "adverse affect" on East-West security talks.[28] Schmidt, while personally opposing a policy of punishment toward the USSR, recognized that human rights issues and electoral problems left him little choice but to join the boycott effort. He insisted, however, that his country's position not be set until closer to the May 24 deadline for accepting Olympic invitations. By that time, he hoped that a common West European position would be worked out.

Genscher continued to serve as the advance man, noting that he was becoming "less sure" that the Federal Republic would send a team to Moscow. He too had to be careful, however, noting that if the Soviets pulled their troops out of Afghanistan his government would lift objections to participation in the Olympics.[29]

The West German Olympic Committee vacillated as much as its government. For it too, Sakharov was the real boycott impetus, even while Afghanistan remained the public test of Soviet behavior. Athletes and officials continued to request governmental support for Olympic participation, but realized that chances for going to Moscow diminished each day Soviet troops remained in Afghanistan, and Sakharov languished in Gorkey.

The West German government had more influence over its sporting authorities than did Mrs. Thatcher. The West Germans did not have a proprietary interest in the Olympic myth, and national political unity clearly was important to even the most ardent of Olympic publicists.

Daume, who probably took his ambitions to succeed Lord Killanin as IOC president into account in forming his position, alternated between threats and pleas. While in Lake Placid, he denounced Carter's alternative games scheme, noting that "counter-Olympics" might cost Los Angeles the 1984 Olympic award.[30] Daume, however, eventually adopted Genscher's formula urging the USSR to "create conditions" that would ensure broad Olympic participation, clearly indicating that, as of the end of February, West Germany probably could not go.[31]

On March 15 Daume, who had so much to lose personally if West Germany boycotted the Olympics, expressed the opinion that the West German Olympic Committee "probably" would accept any government recommendation to boycott the Olympic Games.[32] This was an extremely significant development, reflected not only at the March 22 meeting of European Olympic committees, but also in an East German attack on Daume that included a warning that a West German boycott might harm intra-German sport relations in particular, and political relations in general.[33] The West German Sport Association came out for a boycott the next week.

West Germany did not like being the key to Olympic boycott success, just as it shied away from exposed positions on many important European regional issues. By the middle of March it was clear that West Germany would probably boycott the Games (as evidenced by stepped up Soviet and East German attacks on West Germany policy). The Federal Republic now kept a low profile and waited while other countries settled their decisions.

In France, the strongest West European boycott foe, the Sakharov affair began to demonstrate that general European support for a boycott might be possible. Pre-Sakharov polls showed that the French public discouraged both an Olympic boycott and the idea of a unified European position on Afghanistan. Three-quarters of Frenchmen opposed US policy,[34] even after

130

Sakharov's detention. French Sport Minister Soisson
insisted that France would send a team to Moscow.
Soisson repeated the point on January 26 when he spoke
for all participants in a meeting of Francophone countries.[35] While judging the Soviet invasion of Afghanistan to be "unacceptable," France insisted that an
Olympic boycott was the wrong reaction to it.

While Sakahrov did not affect overall public
opinion, however, elite opinion was significantly
changed. French intellectuals felt far more outraged
at the way Moscow treated this dissident than at the
Afghan invasion. Newspapers such as Le Figaro[36] and
L'Aurore[37] on the right and Le Matin[38] on the left
urged that the West unite behind the boycott move. The
influential, relatively anti-American Le Monde did
not follow this trend, but noted that France might have
to join a boycott if the rest of the West insisted on
it. Two months later even this paper decided, with
great reluctance, to oppose the Moscow Olympics; its
editors believed the stories they heard about alleged
Soviet massacres of Afghan citizens.[39] More importantly,
Le Monde reported that the French government itself had
changed its position, and would urge French sport
authorities to boycott the Olympic Games.

France, despite its feelings on the issue, apparently decided that it had no choice but to contribute
to a unifed European governmental position on the
Games. Assuming that other Eurpean governments could
control their Olympic committees, Paris did not want to
be the only Western country in Moscow. In addition,
the French opposed both superpowers' policies. While
the United States was clumsy, the Soviet Union was in
Afghanistan. Soviet refusal to make any concessions,
either to French pleas or the the British-sponsored
"neutrality" proposal, probably left the French with no
choice. When faced with two rigid superpowers, French
"independence" did not mean very much.

The French Communist Party, of course, professed
support for Soviet policy in Afghanistan, but clearly
was embarrassed by Sakharov's detainment. Party Chief
Georges Marchais had just returned from a trip to
Moscow, on which he underscored the PCF's return from
Eurocommunism to Proletarian Internationalism, when
Moscow moved against the dissident. Marchais' slavishly
pro-Soviet statements on Afghanistan (which were printed
verbatim in the Soviet press[40]) and his televised
meeting with Brezhnev appeared to imply approval of the
Sakharov arrest, something which could only cause great
confusion within the party.

On January 24, the party organ L'Humanite published
a letter from prominent PCF intellectuals strongly
protesting Soviet actions against Sakharov.[41] Whatever
independence the French Communist Party had came from
its legacy of protests over Soviet human rights policy
and the Warsaw Pact intervention in Czechoslovakia in
1968. Having approved the latest Soviet military
adventure, the Party leadership had no choice but to
permit criticism of Sakharov's treatment.

The Italian Communist Party (PCI), on the other
hand, had no qualms about its strong anti-Soviet position on Afghanistan, although both Italian and Spanish
Eurocommunists cautioned that Western actions, such as
NATO theater nuclear force modernization, were as much
to blame for the current international atmosphere as
Afghanistan. The PCI--in much the same terms as the
French government--urged that events in South Asia
needed to be kept in perspective, and that detente had
to be saved. Party leaders decried the Olympic boycott
idea as an "evil and perverse" notion, one which would
discriminate against the Soviet people because of an
error by the Soviet regime.[42]

For its part, the always shaky Italian government
insisted that its Olympic decision would be based on
IOC rulings, and repeated other European government
assurances that the national Olympic committee would
have the last word on participation. This clearly was
not definite, however, since the February and March IOC
statements did nothing to stop Italian efforts to
ascertain the West German position and line up behind
it. Foreign Minister Ruffini and his West German
counterpart issued a joint statement on February 25,
shortly after the twin failures of European Community
and US efforts to form a unified Western Olympic position, affirming the intentions of both governments to
delay their decisions until May 24.[43] Ruffini also
aped Genscher's statement that his country "was at
Washington's side" over Afghanistan, strengthening the
impression that West European governments, in the end,
would support the US Olympic stance. Whether the
Italian government would be able to convince the Italian
Olympic committee to boycott the Games was another
question.

The United Kingdom was in a much different position. Prime Minister Thatcher found that she could not
move sporting officials through persuasion and soon
began to apply direct pressure. Despite previous
promises to respect the right of individual athletes
to go to Moscow, the government let it be known that it
was debating whether to prevent the BBC from covering
the Games, and insisted that British participation in
Moscow would be "catastrophic."[44] The British Olympic

Association, while refraining from immediate acceptance of its Olympic invitation, strongly hinted that it would buck government policy.

The Prime Minister faced another problem. The British royal family was deeply involved in Olympic politics. Prince Philip was president of the International Equestrian Federation; his presence in Moscow would be a special embarrassment to the government. The Prince strongly opposed mixing sport and politics (a curious position given his station in life), but had to go along with the government. He told the press that he might have to contract a convenient illness.[45] His problem was solved when British equestrians voted not to participate in the Games.

In March the Prime Minister applied specific anti-Olympic measures. She banned military athletes from competition, withheld the services of an Olympic attache (an important sanction promising to make life difficult for British athletes in Moscow), and stated that the traditional special leave granted to civil servants who wanted to go to Moscow would be denied.

It was not enough to stop the BOA from going against her. The BOA had money problems, being unable to raise enough funds because of the boycott campaign, but the IOC offer to finance Olympic committees in the BOA's situation helped it keep its position intact. British sporting authorities were not impressed either by government arguments for an alternative games (concentration on this tactic was the worst single mistake made by governments) or by the 315-147 vote in favor of an Olympic boycott by the House of Commons. The latter was arrived at only after some Conservatives criticised their Prime Minister on the grounds that the boycott was not enough, and most of the Labor opposition insisted that it supported BOA independence. About a quarter of the House abstained, denying Thatcher an outright majority. On March 25, the BOA became the first West European Olympic Committee to accept its Olympic invitation. The Prime Minister insisted that the affair was not yet over, but there seemed little she could do.

The BOA noted its hope that its defiance of the government would lead to USOC determination to do the same thing. While US sporting bodies considered their positions, however, the only immediate reaction was from Norway's Olympic Committee, which temporarily reversed its decision to boycott the Olympics. The British decision was not unexpected, and other national Olympic committees had different domestic political considerations, so it had little immediate effect.

Of the other West Europeans, Ireland and Denmark joined France as the strongest opponents of US policy on the Olympics. Both, however, reserved their right to join a boycott if the other Europeans did. Neutrals such as Austria, Sweden, and Finland also opposed a boycott. The first two, however, hedged their Olympic intentions on conditions implying solidarity with the rest of Europe. The latter, because of its special relationship with the Soviet Union, could not afford this luxury. Switzerland also favored Olympic participation, but remembered its 1956 boycott and also looked for a common European solution.

Greece and Spain were special cases. The former wanted to use the issue to become permanent Olympic host; the Greeks had the support of a number of Olympic committees and governments. They needed IOC support for the idea, and therefore were reluctant to support an Olympic boycott. On the other hand, a common European position would expose them to great boycott pressure. In addition, the strongest support for a permanent Greek Olympic home came from the United States, the boycott demanduer.

Athens was also aware that its participation in the Games was made especially sensitive by the Greek tie to Olympic tradition. An Olympic celebration without Greek participation would be embarrassing to an Olympic host, as well as to the IOC. The Greeks showed no sign of denying the Soviets access to the sacred Olympic flame and, doubtless to their relief, nobody brought the subject up.

Madrid, on the other hand, looked beyond the Olympics to the next big public political gathering, the November review of the Helsinki Final Act by participants in the Conference on Security and Cooperation in Europe (CSCE). Spain, the meeting host, very much wanted to prevent the CSCE conference from deteriorating into the kind of polemical donneybrook on human rights that the previous Helsinki review (in Belgrade in 1977-1978) had been. With SALT and other arms control underpinnings of detente in trouble, the CSCE meeting took on a significance greater than its actual clout. The Madrid meeting was to take place in November, just a few months after the Olympics, and the Spanish hinted that perhaps the political atmosphere dictated its postponement.[46] Most other CSCE participants, however, seemed to want the meeting to go on as scheduled. Spain tried to keep a low Olympic profile while it concentrated on CSCE and prepared its appeal to join both NATO and the European Community, a move sure to be opposed by Moscow, and brought up in Madrid.

Other developed Western states looked to the Europeans for their cues on the Olympic boycott, while at
the same time measuring their specific relationships with
both superpowers. Canadian Prime Minister Clark strongly
supported a boycott (after some initial hesitation), but
his Progressive Conservatives were defeated on February
18 by the Liberals and Pierre Elliot Trudeau, who only
supported a boycott on condition of broad support among
third world as well as Western states. The next month
the Canadian Olympic Association voted to go to Moscow
(the Equestrians demurred).

Australia and New Zealand were greatly affected by
the British position. Both governments supported an
Olympic boycott, both Olympic committees did not.
Australian swimmers and the entire New Zealand Olympic
committee (perhaps remembering the 1976 boycott) affirmed
their intentions to defy their governments a few days
before the BOA accepted its invitation to Moscow. The
Australian Labor Party offered to finance Austrialian
athletes if the government refused to.

BOA influence was not as great in other former and
present British dependencies, however. Sports officials
in Bermuda and Hong Kong (the latter in response to the
Chinese as well as British position) both announced pro-
boycott positions after the BOA vote.[47]

Japan, a major gymnastics and volleyball power,
deplored Soviet moves in Afghanistan, but was reluctant--
like everyone else--to embarrass the Soviets through a
public Olympic boycott. The Japanese government remained
in the background of the issue in its early stages,
taking a position only when the Sakharov affair seemed
to solidify feelings in Europe. On January 28 the
government announced that it would make a decision on
February 10, but that its positions would not be binding
on the Japan Olympic Committee (JOC).[48] It soon
became clear that Prime Minister Ohira supported US
policy, and it seemed that Japan would join the boycott
effort.

Tokyo backed off before February 10, however,
because it was clear that European anger over Sakharov
was not going to be translated into an early unanimous
boycott position. The government did come out in favor
of an Olympic boycott, but repeated that this was not
binding on the JOC.[49] Chief Cabinet Secretary Masayoshi
stated that the government would back off its boycott
decision if the Soviets left Afghanistan and responded to
rumors of such a withdrawal with a specific version of
the Genscher formula.[50] Polls taken showed that a majority of Japanese opposed US boycott policy.[51]

Japan, however, was in the same position as the
West Europeans. Public opinion did not matter as much
as the necessity of public solidarity with the United
States. The Olympic boycott was the most public--and the
least costly--means of doing that. In addition, public
opinion, while opposing a boycott, was not so strongly
expressed as to overrule diplomatic considerations.
Japan clearly waited for the other shoe to drop in
Europe.

TOWARD A EUROPEAN POSITION

It appeared that the level of worldwide support for
a boycott of the Moscow Olympic Games depended on the
ability of the West Europeans to agree on a common
boycott position. The Genscher formula, urging that the
Soviets create conditions under which the Games could be
held and implying a boycott if those conditions were
lacking, only held up as long as a decision could be put
off.
In general, Western Europe rejected NATO in favor of
the European Community as a forum for reactions to
Afghanistan, partly because the latter was one step
removed from US influence. On February 5, European
Community foreign ministers adopted the Genscher
formula, leaving the superpowers and themselves maximum
flexibility, while waiting for President Carter to act
on his February 20 deadline.
The next reaction came from the European Parliament,
a largely ceremonial body in which some put renewed hopes
for regional integration as a result of its direct
election by multi-lateral European sufferage in 1979.
On February 15, the Parliament voted to support an
Olympic boycott and to ban sales of surplus commodities
to the USSR. Although the vote carried no weight the
result received a great deal of publicity, and provided
the first evidence of general West European support for
the US position. On February 19 West European
foreign ministers met and tried to forge agreement on
a definite Olympic position. They failed, owing to
French objections to a common boycott stance.
The parliamentary vote and diplomatic efforts at a
common position were overshadowed almost immediately by a
collossal blunder. It is not clear exactly how it
happened, but the US, West German, and French governments
got into a squabble over alleged plans to hold a meeting
between major West European foreign ministers and
Secretary of State Vance. Rumors of the meeting,
allegedly scheduled for Feburary 20 or 21, were floated,
confirmed, and subsequently denied in all directions.
The US declared that the meeting had been set up by
Bonn, and sent Vance to meet with Genscher even though

the other participants refused to get together. Vance
spent the next several days in London and Paris as well
as Bonn, and came home with predictions that all the
West Europeans eventually would join in the boycott
effort.[52] TASS had a field day with the confusion,
noting West European resistance against clumsy, futile,
US pressure.[53]

European national Olympic committees also got
together, and showed no more unity than their governments. On March 22, the British, French, Italian,
Spanish, and four other committees voted to go to Moscow
regardless of government positions. West Germany,
Switzerland, Turkey, the Netherlands, and three others
deferred any decisions pending consultation with government sport authorities. Although polls showed that the
Sakharov affect had largely worn off in Europe,[54] and
that West European publics favored Olympic participation,
at the end of March it appeared that at least West
Germany, and perhaps most other West Europeans, would
boycott the Olympics. On the other hand, Bonn showed
no sign of making its decision before May. No other
West Europeans would get out front of the West Germans,
although Belgian Prime Minister Martens told a Madrid
newspaper that he felt all nine European Community
countries would, in the end, boycott the Olympics.[55]

The issue appeared to be settled when, on April 23,
Chancellor Schmidt announced that his government would
recommend that the West German Olympic committee boycott
the Games. The position the rest of Europe had waited
for was now public, and it seemed inconceivable, in
view of Daume's apparent resignation to the boycott's
inevitability, that the Olympic committee would defy its
government.

Norway reflected a general belief that the boycott
was on by announcing--through yet another vote of the
Olympic committee--that Oslo's team would not go to
Moscow. By May 24, the deadline for accepting Olympic
invitations, most West European governments had called
for boycott support. Although many of them were luke-
warm on the issue, making it clear that they would not
block defiant athletes wanting to attend the Games,
it seemed that most Olympic officials would go along
with government wishes.

It did not work out that way. West European Olympic
committees finally managed to agree on a common strategy,
one that gave them a stronger interest in participation
because it enabled European Olympic officials to rekindle
their flagging Olympic spirit.

In 1980, the Olympic movement clearly lost its will
to beat back the challenge of "politics." The usual
polemics about the lofty aims of sport did not impress

anyone any more. The IOC could not get federations and national committees to allow individuals to buck national boycotts; the basic political content of sport prevented that. Killanin's subsequent visits to Moscow and Washington also proved futile.

Eighteen West European national Olympic committees met in Rome to discuss the situation the first weekend in May. The results of these talks was the May 3 proposal suggesting that committees be permitted to refuse participation in opening Olympic ceremonies and to send teams without national flags, uniforms, or anthems.

Olympic officials stuck to these conditions, believing that these changes would somehow restore the separation of sport and politics. Although this was absurd, it clearly did restore Olympic leaders' faith in Olympic mythology. Agreement to these initiatives--which did reduce the political visibility of West Europeans attending the 1980 Olympics--fueled officials' determination to defy their governments, ignore both Afghanistan and Sakharov, and go to Moscow.

Still, some committees felt that the West German vote would move many other committees, and feared that some federations might defy national Olympic committees and support the Olympic boycott. It is still unclear exactly how the next moves were worked out, but it appears that the French and West German Olympic committees cooperated in a well-conceived attempt to soldify participation momentum.

The French vote was scheduled for May 13, two days before Bonn's and four days after the West German Olympic Committee Praesidium made its recommendation. Suddenly, at that Praesidium meeting, Willi Daume altered his public position and strongly urged that the full committee defy the government and go to Moscow. Although the Praesidium voted 12-7 against him, Daume's appeal signaled a clear intent to reverse West Germany's position.

The French committee followed Daume's turnabout with a decisive pro-Moscow vote. French Olympic officials took advantage of the government's low-keyed suggestion that athletes might not want to attend a "Spartakiade" by ignoring it. The Olympic committee reminded Giscard of his promise that athletes would decide their own fate and the French President, now preparing for his summit with Brezhnev, accepted the vote without complaint.

Daume now insisted that West Germany would be isolated if it boycotted the Games, and hoped that the full West German committee would agree with him. However, unlike in France, the West German government put strong pressure on its Olympic officials not to embarrass it.

The East Germans seriously hurt Daume's cause by clumsily injecting themselves into West German deliberations. East German Olympic chief Manfred Ewald's May 14 conversations with West German sport officials were highly publicized and greatly resented. Daume could not sway powerful federation leaders, and on May 15 the committee voted 59-40 to boycott the Games.

But most West European Olympic Committees followed the French, not the West German model. Paris' decision was not decisive in itself--as each vote was decided on domestic considerations--but important because it assured other committees that they would not be the only West Europeans in Moscow. Only Turkey, Liechtenstein, and Monoco joined West Germany and Norway in voting to boycott.

The rest sent teams, although the latter were seriously reduced by financial problems and individual boycotts by federations and athletes (an important part of the boycott effort, given the destruction of the equestrian, field hockey, yachting, and shooting competitions). The anti-Moscow positions of important West European federations added significantly to the effect of the entire boycott effort, and clearly diluted the West European presence in Moscow.

Nevertheless, Daume spoke of the possibility of West Germany reversing its vote, claiming that his predictions of isolation had been realized. This did not happen, probably because he could not sway federation chiefs in the wake of federation boycotts throughout Europe, and because boycott decisions by most East Asian and moderate Arab countries belied the suggestion that West Germany was isolated. Norway, which had already reversed itself twice, seemed vulnerable to pressure to do so again, but in the end held against Moscow. Following the West European developments, other important developed states split. Australia (by a 6-5 margin) and New Zealand voted to send teams; however, both efforts unraveled as federations and athletes joined the boycott. Individual sport boycotts reduced New Zealand's team from 91 members to four. Japan, the most important actor once the West German result was in, voted 29-13 to stay out of the Olympics.

Neither superpower got what it wanted out of these decisions. The US managed to get West Germany, Japan, and a smattering of others to boycott entirely, and succeeded in gaining the support of important federations in those countries whose NOCs voted to attend the Games. This, plus support elsewhere, assured that the 1980 Olympic Games would have checkered athletic standards and reduced political prestige.

However, the defection of most West European committees from the boycott embarrassed Washington, and raised
questions about Western solidarity. West European
governments never had been enthusiastic about the boycott, but had supported it in order to cheaply buy off
US feelings in the hope that the US then would settle
back into the business of detente. Olympic committee
defiance--and lack of apparent government reaction to
it--meant that there was no common allied response to
Afghanistan. The West Europeans had to brace themselves
for a US reaction that might delay return to detente
until after the Madrid review of the Helsinki Final Act.

For their part, the Soviets expressed glee at the
West European developments, taking them as precisely
the kind of political vindication that West European
Olympic committees denied them to be. Further, Moscow
could point to disarray in the West as a sign that the
"Brezhnev Doctrine" (once communist, always communist)
applied outside Eastern Europe.

On the other hand, US, Japanese, and West German
absence could not be hidden from Soviet sport fans, who
would known how and why the numbers of competitors had
been reduced. The boycott also provided a forum for
the most extensive anti-Soviet publicity in recent
memory, including the unprecedented refusal of most
attending West Europeans to use their national flags
and anthems during the Games. The USSR lost a significant amount of international legitimacy over the
Olympic question, and political legitimacy is what the
Olympics are all about.

THE THIRD WORLD

Third world states, with little or no connection to
the Olympic Movement or its Western origins, had less of
a problem admitting the connection of sport and politics
than the West Europeans. Third world countries are used
to using sport to advertise political legitimacy and,
given US policy on previous boycotts, must have been
amused at President Carter's call to snub Moscow.

The third world was not as hotly contested an arena
as Europe; few developing states had substantial Olympic
teams and none of them had the autonomous Olympic committees that made the West European story so complex. In
addition, most developing states cared little for the
superpower squabble. While the West Europeans hoped to
keep Afghanistan fallout limited to South Asia, most of
the third world wanted to keep the struggle limited to
the superpowers themselves. South Asian countries were
alarmed by Soviet actions, but they did not relish the
thought of American "help."

Still, third world states were courted heavily by both superpowers. The US was aware that its allies wanted maximum global support for an Olympic boycott to provide evidence of universal solidarity against Soviet aggression. France, among others, felt that Afghanistan was more an East-South than an East-West issue. Interestingly, most third world states ignored West European decisions in making their own.

The Soviets prided themselves on being the natural allies of the third world--a contention that Cuba faithfully tried to institutionalize when it chaired the Non-Aligned Movement. The Afghanistan issue threatened to turn third world sentiment against Moscow if Soviet actions were perceived as aggression against a non-aligned state. Broad participation by the developing world in the Olympic Games would dispel such an image in the most public way possible. The USSR offered to pay the way of third world teams to Moscow.

Many third world countries faced an unusual dilemma. Those who were poor in athletic programs as well as in cash probably had no intention of sending a team to Moscow in the first place. Now, because of the Olympic boycott, what was simply a matter of realism might be interpreted as support for an Olympic boycott. Some states played with the idea of sending observers to Moscow, to serve as a political salve to the Soviets while not offending the Americans.

Initial US attention fell on those states most concerned with the Afghan problem, those in South Asia and the Arab world. Kinship through ethnic and religious identification combined with geopolitical fear of Soviet intentions in the Persian Gulf and Indian Ocean to alarm the oil-rich Islamic world. Saudi Arabia, Djibouti, the United Arab Emirates (which later reversed itself), Qatar, and Oman, none of which had Olympic teams in the first place, immediately supported the Olympic boycott. So did Egypt, which had cast its lot with the US and the Camp David process and against Soviet presence in the middle east.

On the other hand, most radical, non-monarchical, and secular Arab states saw little to gain in an Olympic boycott, since they did not see Afghanistan as the major problem in the area. To a certain extent all Arab countries were susceptible to Soviet arguments that Israeli occupation of Arab land, not the Soviet presence in Afghanistan, was the main offense against the Arabs. There was no chance that Syria, Libya, or Algeria would boycott the Olympic Games. Iraq had to balance its dislike of both superpowers' policies, but also seemed unlikely to boycott.

Of the other Islamic states, Iran and Pakistan were
the most important in the Olympic process, since they
were geographically closest to the heart of the problem.*
Iran's President Bani-Sadr made an Olympic boycott part
of his election campaign, perhaps as a cheap, public
method of expressing displeasure with one superpower
while locked in an intense struggle with the other. The
hostage issue, and the bad memories of 25 years of US-
Shah cooperation, nullified any Iranian inclination to
play a major role in Afghanistan question, and boycotting
the Games was the most Iran would do.

Pakistan feared Soviet designs on its Baluchi and
Pushtun populations, and strained to handle its role as
refuge for thousands of Afghans, some of them insurgents.
On the other hand, given disputes with the US over
military aid cut-offs and Pakistan's alleged nuclear
weapons intentions, Pakistan had little interest in a
renewed US alliance. President Zia also had to face the
possibility that Soviet advances, coupled with post-
Vietnam American hestiancy, would make Moscow the one
superpower he had to get along with.

Nevertheless, Pakistan supported the Olympic boycott and pushed it before the January conference of
Islamic states. Given ambivolence toward both superpowers it was somewhat surprising that the conference
issued a fairly strong call to its members to consider
their Olympic positions. Along with the Gulf monarchies
and Pakistan, Malaysia and Indonesia used the conference
to register opposition to the Moscow Olympics.[56]

India, the largest South Asian state, followed a
much different course. Indira Gandhi, recently reelected and more powerful than ever, used the Afghan
issue to reinstate India's special relationship with the
USSR. She accepted--without approval--the Soviet explanation of their actions. Although she did not give
Moscow the overt support it wanted, India strongly and
quickly reaffirmed its intention of participating in the
Olympic Games.[57]

Vietnam and its client states in Laos and Kampuchea,
of course, had no problem supporting Moscow on the
Olympic issue. Thailand and Burma felt pressure from
both superpowers and split their decisions--Thailand
joined the ASEAN (Thailand, Indonesia Malaysia,

---

*It should be noted that parts of the Afghan Olympic team
joined the boycott. The soccer team defected in West
Germany, the basketball team in Pakistan. In April, the
field hockey team, on its way home from a match in
Moscow, was ambushed by rebels. Most of the team was
killed. There were rumors that wrestlers and others
also wanted to defect.

Singapore, Phillipines) boycott of the Olympics while
Burma, after much hesitation, went to Moscow. Pacific
countries such as Papua-New Guinea and Fiji were among
the earliest boycott supporters, expressing their displeasure with Soviet policy in rather strong terms.[58]

Africa was the scene of the most superpower attention in the third world, because African states had
a heritage of Olympic politics and because some of them
had strong Olympic teams. The United States, as a
leader in the opposition to the 1964-1976 African
campaigns against South Africa and Rhodesia, was not in
a good position to push its own boycott position. The
Supreme Council for Sport in Africa (an extremely
effective and well-led organization that coordinated
African use of the Olympic weapon) refused to join
the US campaign, and its stance affected the positions
of African states as much as meetings of national
Olympic committees influenced events in Europe.[59]

The US tried to counteract African skepticism by
assuring, time and time again, that South Africa would
be barred from competing in the alternative games. This
had little effect, since alternative games were as
meaningless to most Africans as to developed states'
Olympic committees.

Certain states did join the boycott efforts, but
because of domestic and international considerations
having nothing to do with alternative games. Zaire, the
largest state on the continent and increasingly
dependent on Western aid, and Liberia, a traditional US
ally, were among the earliest boycott supporters.

Kenya also joined the US camp. Nairobi's position
was of special significance; Kenya had a strong Olympic
tradition and had been the leader of many African boycott efforts, particularly in 1968. President Moi was
concerned about Soviet actions in the horn of Africa
as well as South Asia, and became a leader in the call
for the IOC to move the Olympics from Moscow. Moi, who
received the red carpet treatment on his trip to
Washington in February, used the Olympic issue to pull
his country closer to the United States than at any
time under his predecessor, Jomo Kenyatta.

Zimbabwe was a special case. In a politically
charged epilogue to the old Rhodesia issue, the Mugabe
government applied for admission to the Olympic Games.
This marked the end of Rhodesia and its international
isolation, and the beginning of the effort to mold a
united Zimbabwe. Mugabe used Olympic participation as a
means of rallying support for his government among the
sport-crazy white minority, and of publicizing Zimbabwe's
international legitimacy.

Uganda, at first, said it would not attend the
Olympics, due more to domestic chaos than solidarity with
the US. However, that chaos eventually ensured Ugandan
Olympic participation. A coup brought to power military
officers interested in good relations with Moscow.
Kampala accepted Soviet offers of team subsidation and
took part in the Games.

Nigeria, the most populous black African state and
the other significant actor in the boycott issue, also
sent a team to Moscow. Lagos condemned the Soviet
invasion of Afghanistan, but refused to play a role in
US boycott efforts.

In early February the US tried to bolster its
limited African support by sending boxer Muhammad Ali to
Tanzania, Kenya, Nigeria, Senegal, and Liberia. Ali,
both as a Moslem and a US citizen, was outraged by
Soviet Afghan policy, and was in addition one of the
best known Americans in Africa.

It was a poor move because Ali, for all his stature,
was not a political leader capable of impressing Africans
with how seriously the United States took African
support. In addition, Ali seemed not to have been well-
briefed, either on the politics of international sport
nor on the positions of the countries he was to visit.

This latter problem became acute on his first stop,
Tanzania. President Julius Nyerere, not a sport fan,
was especially insulted at the level of attention Ali
represented and at the fact that Washington sent a boxer
to Africa rather than a diplomat or high-level politi-
ian. Tanzanians pressed the boxer with questions about
lack of US support for African boycott efforts. Ali,
clearly impressed with his questioners, answered that
he was not an "Uncle Tom," and promised to reexamine his
boycott position.[60]

Ali felt better in Kenya and Liberia, already com-
mitmed to the boycott, and in Senegal, which did not yet
take an active role in the question. Nigeria, however,
reacted like Tanzania. President Shagari refused to
meet Ali, and Lagos reaffirmed what had been a tentative
intention to participate in the Olympics. Shagari pegged
his position to that of the Supreme Council for Sport in
Africa, however, thus leaving himself an out should
continental support for a boycott coalesce.[61]

In Latin America there was originally even less
support for the boycott; Afghanistan was far away and the
United States, not the USSR, was the superpower feared in
the hemisphere. "Human rights" conjured up not Sakharov,
but US demands on various Latin American governments.
While some Latin American states simply sought to demonstrate independence from the United States, others used
the public and peripheral nature of the Olympic Games

to polish their "progressive" credentials. Only Chile,
perhaps in response to the Soviet boycott of a soccer
match shortly after the fall of Salvador Allende in 1973,
immediately came out for an Olympic boycott.

Cuba, of course, followed the Soviet line, attacking the United States both for its boycott policy and
for its general international perfidy. Teofilo
Stevenson, Cuba's most famous boxer, insisted that the
boycott movement could mean the end of the Olympics.[62]

Mexico was even more vocal than Cuba since it did
not have the former's handicap of appearing to be
enslaved to the Soviet line. Mexico hosted the Association of National Olympic Committees when this body voted
to go to Moscow. Its own Olympic committee, strongly
supported by the government, insisted that Mexico would
send a team. The Mexicans made no mention of the 1968
events, choosing instead to repeat simple Olympic
mythology.

The Games turned out badly for Mexico, however, as
its fans perceived Warsaw Pact diving judges to have
cheated a Mexican diver out of a gold medal. The incident caused mass demonstrations in front of the Soviet
embassy in Mexico City. This sort of traditional
Olympic politics would have happened regardless of
Afghanistan, but the boycott issue increased Soviet
embarrassment over Mexican complaints.

Brazil, Colombia, Peru, and Argentina originally
took positions favorable to the Olympic Games. Brazil
and Colombia seemed content to permit Olympic participation without much official government comment. Peru,
like Mexico, was more vocal in its support of the Moscow
Olympics. Argentina, probably influenced more by the
West German than US position, eventually joined the boycott.

THE BOYCOTT IN PERSPECTIVE

The Games themselves went ahead with the usual level
of pomp and politics. The boycott's effect on standards
of play varied from sport to sport. Those already
mentioned, such as yachting, field hockey, and equestrian events, were decimated by the absence of traditional athletic powers. Basketball was also seriously
impaired by the US boycott. The glamor sports of
swimming and track and field were less seriously affected, at least in terms of the number of records set.
Still, in some events, leading competitors swam against
the clock or struggled for a distance, rather than
against a competitive field. Weightlifting and wrestling were among the least diluted by the boycott.

Women's gymanstics was a special case. Not only
were there the usual judging problems (one could not
call them "irregularities"), but it appeared that there
may have been some premeditation in the gold medal split
among Warsaw Pact athletes. In addition, the perform-
ances of the leading female gymanasts did not seem to
be on a par with the spectacular exhibitions of previous
Olympiads.

The 1980 Olympic boycott did not succeed in moving
the Olympic Games from Moscow. However, the absence of
nearly 65 teams (perhaps 55 because of the boycott)
robbed from Moscow the sense of international legitimacy
that the Games normally provide the Olympic host. There
was no way for the Soviet government to hide from its
people the depth of anger over Afghanistan, nor to
embellish an event now largely reduced to the level of
a Warsaw Pact inter-army games. This does not mean that
Soviet citizens began to question government policy,
only that they knew that many countries doubted Soviet
explanations of it.

The boycott did not do anything to get Soviet
troops out of Afghanistan--no one promoting it ever
thought it would--but it did provide a medium for
appropriate public expression of the deterioration of
superpower relations. It might have provided a potent
reaction to Soviet dissident policy, had the United
States chosen to stress Helsinki-related implications of
the relationship of dissidents and Soviet Olympic
preparation. To this observer it certainly provided
evidence that the political competition inherent in the
Olympic system is as interesting as the athletic contests themselves.

The qualified success of the boycott contrasted
sharply with the West's complete failure to coordinate
other reactions to Afghanistan. The Olympics were
certainly the most public of sanctions, but also the
most peripheral. The Games ended on August 3 and
Western response to Afghanistan and other irritants
quickly became reduced to rhetoric and posturing. The
great failure surrounding Western Olympic policy was the
inability to weave the boycott into a coherent strategy
of response to Soviet actions abhored throughout the
Atlantic Alliance.

NOTES

1. Goodhart and Chataway, War Without Weapons,
p. 128.
2. China Sport, April, 1962, p. 2.
3. China Sport, June, 1962, p. 1.
4. Goodhart and Chataway, War Without Weapons,
p. 129.

146

5. <u>Washington Post</u>, April 8, 1979.
6. <u>Ibid.</u>
7. William Armbruster, "Taiwan's 'Niet' to Naval
Base," <u>Far Eastern Economic Review</u>, XCIII, #34 (August
20, 1976), p. 27.
8. Galia Golan, "The Soviet Union and the PLO,"
<u>Adelphi Papers</u> #131 (London: International Institute
of Strategic Studies, 1976).
9. <u>Reuter</u>, July 22, 1980.
10. <u>Reuter</u>, February 10, 1980.
11. <u>Pravda</u>, March 18, 1980.
12. <u>Reuter</u>, March 27, 1980.
13. <u>Romana Libera</u> (Bucharest) July 25, 1980.
14. <u>Scinteia</u> (Bucharest) July 26, 1980, <u>Pravda</u>
July 27, 1980.
15. <u>Izvestiya</u>, February 20, 1980.
16. <u>New York Times</u>, December 19, 1979.
17. <u>Izvestiya</u>, January 11, 1980.
18. <u>Daily Telegraph</u> (London) January 22, 1980.
19. <u>Frankfurter Rundschau</u>, January 22, 1980.
20. Hamburg, ARD Television, January 21, 1980.
21. <u>Le Soir</u> (Brusdels), November 16, 1979.
22. <u>Reuter</u>, January 25, 1980.
23. <u>Deutsche Press Agentur</u> (DPA), January 25, 1980.
24. <u>DPA</u>, February 15, 1980.
25. <u>DPA</u>, February 21, 1980.
26. <u>Dow Jones</u>, March 6, 1980.
27. <u>Associated Press</u> (AP), March 6, 1980.
28. <u>DPA</u>, March 9, 1980.
29. <u>DPA</u>, March 11, 1980.
30. <u>United Press International</u> (UPI), February
24, 1980.
31. Deutschlandfunk Network, February 25, 1980.
32. <u>DPA</u>, March 15, 1980.
33. East German International Service, March
16, 1980.
34. Paris Domestic Service, January 27, 1980.
35. <u>Ibid.</u>
36. <u>Le Figaro</u>, January 28, 1980.
37. <u>L'Aurore</u>, January 22, 1980.
38. <u>Le Matin</u>, January 22, 1980.
39. <u>Le Monde</u>, March 14, 1980.
40. <u>TASS</u>, January 22, 1980.
41. <u>L'Humanite</u>, January 24, 1980.
42. <u>L'Unita</u>, February 2, 1980.
43. <u>AP</u>, February 25, 1980.
44. <u>Reuter</u>, February 5, 1980.
45. <u>UPI</u>, March 10, 1980.
46. <u>El Pais</u> (Madrid), March 23, 1980.
47. <u>Reuter</u>, March 27, 1980, <u>UPI</u>, March 26, 1980.
48. <u>Reuter</u>, January 28, 1980.

49. Tokyo Kyodo, February 1, 1980, February 2, 1980.

50. Tokyo Kyodo, February 9, 1980.

51. Asahi Shimbun, March 10, 1980.

52. Reuter, February 22, 1980.

53. TASS, February 24, 1980.

54. Washington Post, March 29, 1980.

55. ABC (Madrid), March 20, 1980.

56. Reuter, February 7, 1980.

57. Agence France Press, January 25, 1980.

58. Reuter, January 29, 1980.

59. Accra Domestic Service, January 23, 1980.

60. UPI, February 4, 1980.

61. Reuter, February 8, 1980.

62. Reuter, January 27, 1980.

8 | Los Angeles and Beyond

The Afghanistan issue shows how hard it is to predict which political events will dominate future Olympic Games. It is certain that the next Olympic celebrations will reflect their political environment, but the following speculations on specific problems is meant only as a preliminary guide to political sport over the next few years.

1984

In Sarajevo the IOC has picked another potential Olympic hot spot. Yugoslavia is rent with ethnic ferment and, with Tito's death, could conceivably face political ferment endangering the federation's existence. Thus far, the leadership transition has been orderly. It is still unclear how well Tito's successors will handle Serbo-Croatian rivalry, Yugoslavia's difficult relationship with Bulgaria, and other problems. It is to be hoped that the Balkans will be quieter during the 1984 winter Olympics than when the Archduke of Austria-Hungary paid a visit to Sarajevo seventy years earlier.

Los Angeles brings other considerations to mind. While Moscow was embarrassed by the turmoil surrounding the 1980 Olympic Games, it is far from clear that the Soviets will respond with a boycott of the Los Angeles Olympics. The old Soviet-American rivalry has been rekindled by the boycott issue, but at this point it seems doubtful that its heat will carry over four years. Soviet-American relations in sport usually reflect the current political atmosphere, as the shift in mood from 1952 to 1956 will attest. It is too soon to tell what that mood will be in 1984.

Of the major international problems, Korea presently seems most likely to affect the Los Angeles Games (the South Africa and China issues appear to be settled, and there is no chance that the United States would keep Israel out of the Games). Recently the North Koreans

have undertaken a diplomatic offensive designed to
change their image as orphans in international politics.
Part of this campaign has been an attempt to absorb
South Korean teams in "unified" sport. South Korea
was invited to participate in the 1980 Pyongyang World
Table Tennis Championships. North Korea offered to
negotiate toward a unified 1980 Olympic team, and has
shown some interest in creating single Korean sport
federations. Seoul has so far reacted negatively to
all of this, perhaps seeing it as a trick, as an admission of North Korean cultural isolation, or as part of
the complicated game Pyongyang plays with Moscow and
Peking. The last time the two Koreas tried to get
together was before the 1964 Olympics, a move which was
aborted by North Korea's absence from the Tokyo Games as
a result of its support for GANEFO. It is possible that
there will be some negotiations for a unified Korean
team in 1984. The Sino-Soviet political/military
balance and the fluid South Korean political situation
will significantly affect Pyongyang's Olympic policy.

At present, it seems possible that US domestic
problems could dominate the political centent of the
Los Angeles celebration. Harry Edwards, and others
involved in the abortive attempt to organize a black
boycott of the 1968 US Olympic team might see Los
Angeles as an opportunity to try again. Many who
argued before the Mexico City Games that American blacks
were exploited in political sport have since seen no
reason to change their minds. The US, as Olympic host,
would be especially vulnerable to any significant boycott effort, both in terms of team quality and international publicity.

In addition, of course, 1984 is a presidential
election year, and the national political conventions
probably will fall close to the dates of the Games. If
the two circuses overlap it will be interesting to see
which one gets more television time and the larger
national audience.

Herbert Hoover probably made a mistake when he
ignored the potential publicity of the 1932 Olympic
opening ceremony; neither the Democratic nor Republican
candidate is likely to do the same. Candidates for
office within California probably will deluge Olympic
facilities, as will congressional hopefuls from US medal-
winners' home districts. It is likely that any Olympic
heroes who decide to back one candidate or another will
be whisked into the political arena in short order. Some
Olympic champions might even use the Games to launch
political careers of their own.

A more serious problem could arise if Puerto Rico--
the nexus of US domestic and international policy--
becomes an issue in 1984. Hollywood's second chance for
Olympic celebration is also a potential site for demonstrations by those favoring Puerto Rican Olympic and
political separation from the United States.

Puerto Rico, as one of the few sub-state Olympic
actors, gains a special sort of political legitimacy
from Olympic participation. Puerto Rico's Olympic
committee voted to support the 1980 Olympics, leaving
it to each federation whether athletes would go to
Moscow. The small Puerto Rican team at the 1980 Olympics
provided an embarrassing breach of the boycott, particularly because it ensured participation in the Games by
US nationals without dual citizenship.

The separatist movement on Puerto Rico has been
floundering. Despite President Carter's recent pardon
of individuals involved in attacks on members of Congress
in the 1950's, the separatists lack both publicity and
adherents, and their activities remain largely confined
to scattered bombings on the mainland. This could
change dramatically if athletes sympathetic to Puerto
Rican independence choose to use the Games to give their
cause its greatest possible international publicity.
This scenario will increase in likelihood if the present
campaign for Puerto Rican statehood fails.

OLYMPIC REFORM?

The 1980 Olympic boycott has triggered repetition of
most of the reform suggestions periodically raised
regarding the Olympic Games. Most of these ideas are
meant to remove politics from sport, until now a futile
preoccupation.

Juan Antonio Samaranch, the new IOC president, is
certainly in a better position to deal with the Olympic
Movement's political and diplomatic problems than his
predecessor. Samaranch, an industrialist and long-time
official in Spanish sport organization, was ambassador
to the USSR during the 1980 Games. Presumably, he
represented both his country and the IOC during the
Olympic imbroglio. He seems less sanguine that Killanin
as to the prospects for the separation of sport and
politics (Killanin, for his part, certainly was more
realistic on this score than Avery Brundage).

Nevertheless, Samaranch presides over an organization which remains steeped in mythology and continues to
lose control over international sport. Monique Berlioux,
the redoubtable IOC Executive Director and power behind
the Olympic throne, seems determined to protect Olympic
lore. It is doubtful that anything can reverse the
steady erosion of IOC power in international sport.

The IOC's proceedings during the boycott controversy clearly annoyed many federation heads, who not
only differed over the question of anti-boycott tactics,
but became impatient with the lack of direction Killanin
and his colleagues showed during the struggle. Thomas
Keller, President of the General Assembly of Sport
Federations, several times expressed disappointment with
the IOC's handling of the Moscow Olympics, and strongly
hinted that the federations will play a greater role
in the future of international sport. The failure of
the IOC to preserve unity among national Olympic committees and sport federations during the boycott campaign
certainly was evidence of fragmentation in the Olympic
system and petrification of the IOC.

It is doubtful that the specific reform proposals
raised in 1980 would, if adopted (which is generally
unlikely) have much effect on political sport or on the
continuing diminution of IOC authority. Nevertheless,
certain ideas are worth comment.

The most publicized thought is that the Games should
have a permanent host, or else revolve between several
"neutral" sites, (in political terms). Greece, once
more, is the most widely supported potential host. The
IOC side-stepped the issue in 1980, putting it off to
its 1981 meeting in Baden-Baden, West Germany. It is
estimated that a permanent Olympic site could be constructed by 1992.

The IOC, in considering this proposal, will have to
decide whether or not to surrender its major political
function--the choice and supervision of Olympic hosts--
for the sake of what would be a private amusement park
and convention center. Athens has offered to make the
new site international, and the IOC certainly has--or can
raise--the capital needed for Olympic construction. If
IOC members can be satisifed with a magnificent country
club and museum of ancient Olympic lore, the Greek site
should do quite well.

However, permanent site selection will not separate
sport and politics. For one thing, Greece is not
neutral. Although its NATO membership should not be a
problem, its chronic differences with Turkey would be.
Cyprus, questions of sovereignty in the Aegean, and
basic Greco-Turkish cultural animosity would loom over
Olympic celebrations. A Greek site would involve
political considerations reminiscent of the 1896
Olympics and similar to other Olympic locations, should
Greco-Turkish difficulties erupt during an Olympic year.

More importantly, states will celebrate their physical specimens and political systems at a permanent
Olympic site as easily as under the present system. As
long as national teams, flags, and anthems are kept as

pillars of the Olympic structure, the same problems
inherent in political identification between fan and
athlete will continue.

Some people, with an eye to these problems, are
suggesting complete abandonment of national units. However, as noted several time in this analysis, the IOC has
consistantly rejected this in the past and probably would
do so again. Even if the IOC favored this approach it is
doubtful that it would have any success bucking national
Olympic committees, who would lose their power if international sport no longer was organized along national
lines. The IOC simply is not powerful enough to adopt a
non-national structure, and the federations have so far
shown no interest in it.

Team sports could be eliminated in order to damp
down some of the most nationalistic Olympic celebrations,
but the other sports would still provide plenty of
political action. The IOC could also consider competition between multi-national teams in order to defuse
national identification. This would meet with national
Olympic committee disapproval, however, and would also
present linguisitic and logistical difficulties.

It would be possible to reduce some of the problems
posed by political judging if all sports not decided by
time, distance, or head-to-head racing were removed from
the Olympic program. Figure skating, gymnastics, and
other sports with subjective judging always provide a
forum for political squabbles. However, these sports are
popular, and their political content certainly would
continue to affect world championships, if not the
Olympics themselves. The federations in charge of these
sports would oppose exclusion from the most prestigious
international sporting event, and the federations as a
whole probably would block any IOC efforts to alter the
Olympic program on political grounds.

It may be that there is nothing wrong with the
Olympic System as it is. Perhaps the only thing making
it seem like a problem exists is the belief that there
must be a separation of sport and politics. If so, the
world's spectators, by simply ignoring Olympic mythology
and Olympic apologists, can settle back and prepare to
enjoy a system in which political events are as interesting as sporting endeavor.

On the other hand, if one assumes that the present
preoccupation with sport as a political tool is un-
healthy, a more general overhaul of the Olympic Movement
may be in order. In that case, reformers should start
by reconsidering the basic assumption behind the Olympic
system. Competitive sport is not necessarily a special
form of intercultural transaction helping to mold
attitudes conducive to international understanding.
Perhaps sport is not an especially effective way to bring

the adult world into miniature for the benefit of impressionable adoloscents. Sport may not really serve even as an educational experience for gifted amateurs.

In short, it may be necessary to jettison the baggage of Thomas Arnold and Pierre de Coubertin in order to encourage a realistic adjustment of the Olympic system. The vast resources of the IOC could then be channeled away from sport, perhaps toward some sort of intercultural learning center (or centers) where the youth of the world could study international problems, rather than celebrate them, and where sport would be merely one of many forms of cultural polinization.

Of course, this would still not separate politics from sport. The federations still would provide the kind of political competition that states and spectators want. World championships would stand out as the premier showcase for political sport. Many athletes would still be trapped in a holding pattern where they would spend their post-Olympic lives training their successors, rather than moving on to the real-life productivity originally envisioned for them by Olympic founders.

Without such an overhaul, the IOC probably will go to Sarajevo and Los Angeles with much the same mythology and organization as before. As long as the world pays court to representative international political competition the sport system will continue to thrive on the rich mixture of sport and politics.

Cultural exchange involves those international relations undertaken in order to expose people to systems different than their own. The process of exchange is the purpose of exchange. This almost functionalist aura has been reinforced in sport by Olympic mythology contending separation of sport from its political environment. Nevertheless, in future Olympic Games, as well as other sporting events, political considerations will be as relevent and as important as athletic spectacle. Political sport serves to remind us that international relations, no matter how secretly conducted, are bound to mass publics who, in the final analysis, serve as both audience and judge of those who lead them.

Index

158